The Art of Jewelry Design

The Art of
Jewelry Design
Principles of Design, Rings and Earrings

Text by Maurice P. Galli
in collaboration with Nina Giambelli

Illustrations by Maurice P. Galli, Fanfan Li and Dominique Rivìere

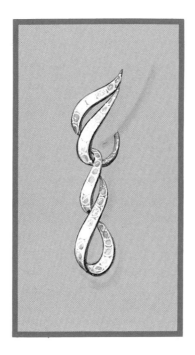

4880 Lower Valley Road, Atglen, PA 19310

Acknowledgements

We would like to thank the following people for their encouragement, advice, and support of this book project: Mr. John Loring, Senior Vice President and Design Director of Tiffany & Co.; Professor Samuel Beizer, Chairman of the Jewelry Design Department at F.I.T.; Mr. Ambaja Shinde, Head Designer at Harry Winston; Mr. Peter G. Scotese, Chairman of the Board of Trustees at F.I.T.; Mr. David Finn, of Ruder-Finn; Ms. Ginger Dick, an international jewelry writer; Mr. André Chervin, of Carvin French.

We are particularly grateful to Esther Park, for generously volunteering her time to type the first drafts of the text, to Carol Bohdan for her advice, and to Larry Wojick for his contribution of a technical illustration.

We would also like to thank Nina Giambelli for her invaluable help in finding a publisher, and for her knowledgeable collaboration in revising the text.

Published by Schiffer Publishing Ltd.
4880 Lower Valley Road
Atglen, PA 19310
Phone: (610) 593-1777; Fax: (610) 593-2002
E-mail: Info@schifferbooks.com
Please visit our web site catalog at **www.schifferbooks.com**

In Europe, Schiffer books are distributed by Bushwood Books
6 Marksbury Avenue Kew Gardens
Surrey TW9 4JF England
Phone: 44 (0) 20-8392-8585; Fax: 44 (0) 20-8392-9876
E-mail: info@bushwoodbooks.co.uk
Free postage in the UK. Europe: air mail at cost.

This book may be purchased from the publisher.
Include $3.95 for shipping. Please try your bookstore first.
We are always looking for people to write books on new and related subjects.
If you have an idea for a book please contact us at the above address.
You may write for a free catalog.

Foreword

Jewelry Design as a phrase, a book title, a discipline, or a college degree, brings up many images. Most of them totally different from each other. A book of Art-Deco Jewelry Design will have photographs of beautiful jewelry from that period. A book of Artist's Jewelry designs will have photographs of unusual designs by famous and lesser known artists-cum-jewelers from the last 150 years. Other books on how to create jewelry designs, or on the creation of jewelry, really deal with the actual making of the finished product from the raw materials, gold, silver, diamonds, etc.

While these and other books are excellent in terms of both teaching the process as well as research into the past and present existing designs in all areas of jewelry, none of the many current books on jewelry design discuss the most important aspect of design: Where does it come from? How is the concept created? In what manner does the movement and arrangement of little pieces of precious material come together.

That aspect of jewelry design, the creative process, has always been part of the mystique, the mystery, the unknown in jewelry design. We look at the works of Faberge, Cartier, Donald Claflin, David Webb. We know they exist. We have seen the final product. Any scholar can deconstruct the actual pieces and show the antecedents of Art Nouveau, Lalique, Retro, Art-Deco, etc. But few people have a clue as to the process.

This new book, written by Maurice Galli, head designer at Tiffany, Fanfan Li, designer at Van Cleef and Arpels, and Dominique Rivière, designer at GemVeto, takes up this daring challenge. The three authors representing some of the best jewelry houses in the world, have refined the essence of the creative process in jewelry in a clear, understandable, comprehensive manner. There is none of the jargon of many other books purporting to deal with the creative process. As designers, they have used colors, paints and brushes, to teach in detail how to approach the design of jewelry.

It is a book that I have searched for, in vain, for many years. It is both the first and undoubtedly the best, and will remain the best for many years. This book is destined to become the bible of the designer, the guide of the artisan, and the companion of the jewelry lover.

Samuel Beizer, Chairman, Jewelry Design,
Fashion Institute of Technology

Contents

THE EARRING

Introduction

Our primary purpose in this book is to explore the creative process and techniques involved in the realization of the Jewel, from the concept to the initial sketch, to the fully evolved rendering. To date, no comprehensive book has ever been published on the methodologies of designing and rendering jewelry.

This book has been conceived as a handbook and reference, especially for instructors and students, delineating all aspects of design in a step by step progressive fashion -- through illustrations.

In order to afford the reader a familiarization with the different topics, the book has been divided into three distinct parts. Part I deals with the basic principles of design, perspective, composition, and documentary studies, and Part II covers metal and stone rendering techniques. In Parts I & II, the technical points are analyzed at length both in the text and graphic examples. Part III offers a valuable source of reference and inspiration through extensive illustrations of specific jewel types and styles. The book has been divided into two volumes. The first volume includes Parts I & II, and Rings and Earrings, of Part III, two of the eight jewelry categories covered. Volume II contains Brooches, Bracelets, Necklaces, Tiaras, Watches, Accessories, and Avant-garde jewelry. It also implements the principles and techniques covered in the first two sections, and features a more concise text related to generic principles applying to jewelry, and includes references and helpful hints, such as the "variation on a basic shape," a recurrent theme indicating a cost progression of a single design concept.

Creativity is a never ending search for new approaches to old problems. It reflects, in the process, the changing social and aesthetic trends, in its effort to differentiate yesterday from today, and tomorrow from yesterday. This ongoing quest must, if it is to be successful, be sustained by a sound knowledge of the fundamental teachings of the past.

We have endorsed these ideas in our respective careers and hope that they will be useful to our students as they have been to us.

Part I
Basic Principles of Design
& Documentary Studies

PART I.

PLATE 1. BASIC TOOLS

Plate 1 illustrates some of the basic tools required for jewelry design. The following list itemizes the materials used and recommended for the basic techniques covered in the text and illustrations:

MECHANICAL PENCIL: LEAD HOLDER for Fine Line Leads (.3m/m to .7m/m)
LEADS (assortment from soft to hard leads)
BEROL PRISMACOLOR Pencils:
#949 Silver
#938 White
#935 Black
FOR DESIGN TRANSFER:
Metal BURNISHER
Metal Point (heavy sewing needle)
PAPER:
CANSON Vellum Tracing Paper (50 wt.)
CANSON gray paper (18" x 24" sheets)
COLOR AID (assorted colors)
BRUSHES: WINSOR & NEWTON "Series 7" Sable (assortment from #0 to #4)
COLOR PALETTE:
PELIKAN GRAPHIC WHITE
GRUMBACHER "Symphonic Brilliant Water Colors #30/17"
WINSOR & NEWTON Designers Gouaches:
NAME # SERIES
Cadmium Primrose 583 4
Golden Yellow 574 3
Cadmium Yellow Deep 586 4
VanDyck Brown 534 1
Jet Black 514 1
Neutral Tint 032
LeFRANC & BOURGEOIS "LINEL": Monaco Yellow 2
VARNISH: LeFRANC & BOURGEOIS varnish for gouache
MISCELLANEOUS:
Erasing Shield
Kneaded Erasure
Sandpad
Rulers
Small and Large BOW COMPASS (circles from 1/37" to 7", and to 15")
Dividers
2 triangles 30/60, 6" and 8"
Paper stumps (assortment)
Drafting tape
Paint palettes (plastic or ceramic)

PLATE 2. BASIC SHAPES & ELEMENTARY PRINCIPLES OF COMPOSITION

Let us begin our approach to the creative process through the simplest forms. Plate 2 illustrates five of the most basic shapes used in three compositions. Here, we are entering a two- dimensional field. The elements, in the shape of squares, rectangles, triangles, circles and trapezoids, provide a satisfactory basis for the design. Visual interest will be obtained through two basic methods: variation in size and overlapping of the elements.

In composition "A," the triangle is the dominant shape, though this may not be so apparent in the horizontal pattern created by the overlapping of the square, rectangle and large circle. Although two-dimensional, a feeling of depth is created by the overlapping of elements: the rectangle on the top plane, followed by the large circle and square, and the triangle on the bottom plane. The small circle on top assures the lightness of the composition. These elements are carefully balanced and juxtaposed to form a harmonious composition, and it is this kind of equilibrium which must be established to create a sound design.

Compositions "B" and "C" do not rely on a single dominant shape, but, rather, on the use of three larger shapes: the square, triangle and circle. In these compositions, the contrast is obtained by the smaller shapes, and the overlapping creates the feeling of depth while eliminating any heaviness in the overall design.

Relative to our previous comments, Composition "D" is a perfect example of what not to do. The overlapping of elements identical in shape, size and weight will not redeem the resulting heaviness, nor will the aesthetic sense react positively toward the dullness of this particular design.

The most intricate compositions, once analyzed, can always be reduced to their basic elements, and these are, by definition, of a simple nature. We will further demonstrate this point in the following plate.

Packing Slip

RETURN ADDRESS:

B&N.COM Customer Returns
1 Barnes & Noble Way
Monroe Township, NJ 08831

Within the United States: 1-800-THE-BOOK

SOLD TO:	SHIP TO:	CUSTOMER SERVICE:
DOTTIE WINKE 206 2ND ST NW WAUKON, IA 521721617 UNITED STATES	DOTTIE WINKE 206 2ND ST NW WAUKON, IA 521721617 UNITED STATES	To Reach Customer Service e-mail : web customers: service@barnesandnoble.com

CUST NO: 23229252   ORDER NO:132317371   **Loc: 44CH4256**

QTY	DESCRIPTION	ITEM #	LIST PRICE	OUR PRICE	TOTAL
1	Art of Jewelry Design: Principles of Design, Rings and Earrings	9780887405624		40.46	40.46

**FREE Shipping on nook, the hot new eBook Reader.
Order Yours Today!
NEW! Write a review on bn.com for a chance to win
a dream vacation! No purchase necessary to enter
or win. See Official Rules and complete details
at www.bn.com/reviews.**

**Please note - sales tax for
the state of IA was
collected on this order.**

If you are not satisfied with your
order, you may return it within
14 days of the delivery date.
For your convenience, items
may be returned to the address
on the packing slip or returned
to your local Barnes & Noble
store (check the local store
refund policy for details).

PayMethod: MC
CreditCard#: 5450

4401013231737110101
(99031000000105770219)

04/29/2010 12:00AM (CL)

From:

DOTTIE WINKE

DOTTIE WINKE
206 2ND ST NW
WAUKON, IA 521721617
UNITED STATES

To:

Barnes & Noble.com
B&N.COM Customer Returns
1 Barnes & Noble Way
Monroe Township, NJ 08831
USA

4401013231737110101

Barnes & Noble.com

9903100000105770219
(4401013231737710101)

Express Delivery

4/29/2010 8:51:26AM

return instructions

REASON FOR RETURN (PLEASE CHECK ONE)

○ Damaged in Transit   ○ Defective   ○ Wrong Quantity

○ Wrong Merchandise Received   ○ Other
(explain below)

COMMENTS: _____

_____

_____

_____

_____

FOR RETURNS: PLEASE CUT OUT LABEL ON DOTTED LINE AND ADHERE TO CARTON BEING RETURNED

QTY	DESCRIPTION	ITEM #	UNIT PRICE	AMOUNT

TOTAL

PLEASE ADD APPLICABLE POSTAGE

For your own protection we suggest you return items UPS or insured parcel post. Should the items be lost or damaged in transit, carriers require that you file the tracer or claim. Postage is non-refundable.

PLATE 3. ANALYSIS OF A BROOCH

In Plate 3, we have chosen a typical Art Deco brooch to illustrate the use of basic forms in design. To emphasize the structural aspect, the various forms have been isolated so as to present them in their sheer simplicity. The circular forms are predominant, and the elongated rectangles are used as contrasting elements to relieve the weight of the circles and underline their respective positions.

In the composition, a strong sense of balance is created by the powerful forms. Having established a preliminary concept, three decorative elements are introduced in the form of polished metal, black enamel and diamond pavé surfaces. The decorative value of each element is determined by texture, color and form. The highly polished aspect of silver or platinum contrasts with the depth of the black enamel, while the diamond elements add richness to the whole, asserting the precious nature of the object.

An aspect of this design that should be emphasized is the balance of color versus texture. As a general rule, elements of similar shapes and dimensions will, through the use of various colors or textures, acquire different visual weights, i.e., a dark color or coarse texture will visually be more heavy.

Plate 3 illustrates two designs based on elements derived from the original brooch. The well-proportioned dimensions of these elements made our work relatively easy. It is indeed the nature of good designs to lend themselves to numerous interpretations. These interpretations can be a valuable exercise for students.

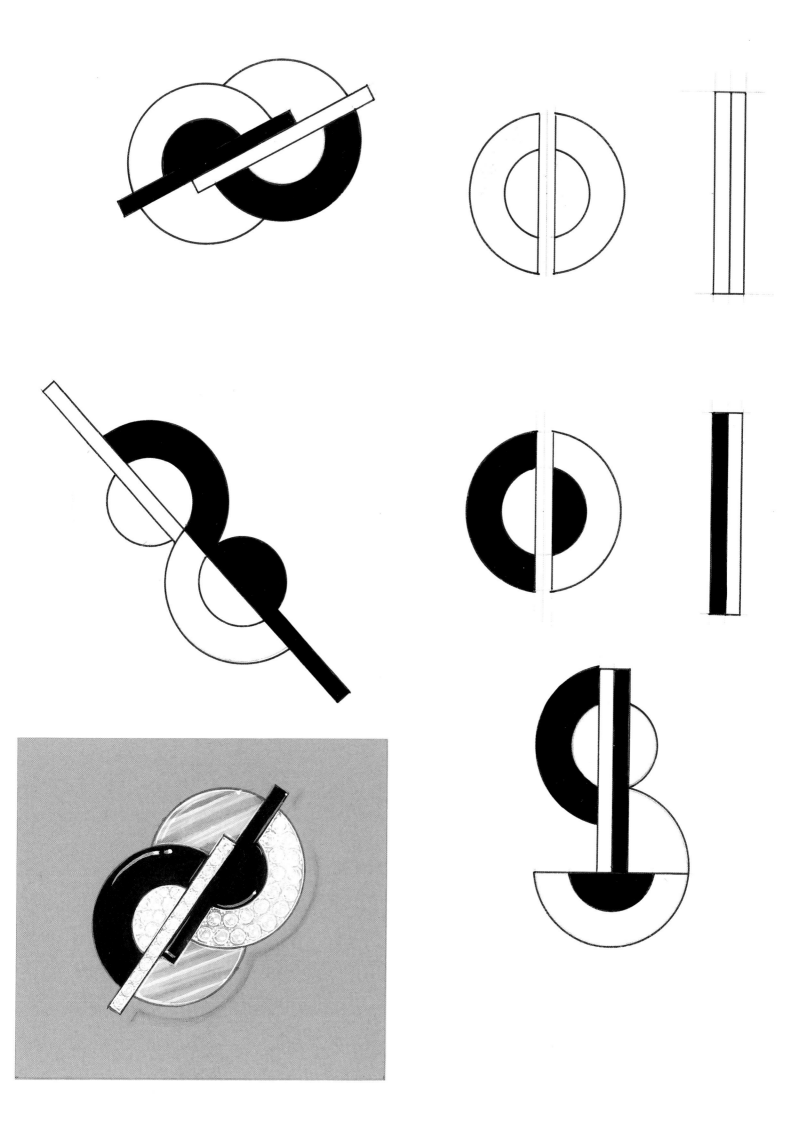

PLATE 4. VISUAL WEIGHT: Values & Contrasts

We will now study values in design. A value can best be described as the graduation of a gray tone from light to dark, white to black.

Figure #1 illustrates the progression from white to black in four basic values. The possibility of extending such a graduation is easily understandable.

An important factor related to the use of values is their contrasting properties. In Figure #2, the first two squares (#1 & #2) display contrasting values, creating a powerful visual impact. As an aside, let us point out an unusual optical effect: the small white square (#1), appears somewhat larger in dimension than the small black square (#2).

Square #3, by comparison with the other two, does not offer a drastic contrast. The black takes on a grayish appearance due to the small gray square set in its center, creating a softer visual impact. Such delicate contrasts in which closely related colors and/or values are used give an understated look to the jewel.

The simulated necklaces show the variations of values exemplified by the placement of high and low visual weights. In the lower necklace, the strongest visual weight is placed at the center by way of the black triangle, which allows the eye to focus and visually anchor the composition. This type of symmetrical layout calls for a central focus and whenever this expectation is not met, the composition becomes weak. The other necklace exemplifies this weakness. With the lighter value at its center, the composition lacks a central focus and the eye drifts back and forth between the black triangles. The placement of visual weight is equally important with asymmetrical designs, as in the earring layouts at the top, where the pitfall of misplaced weight is seen in the example on the left.

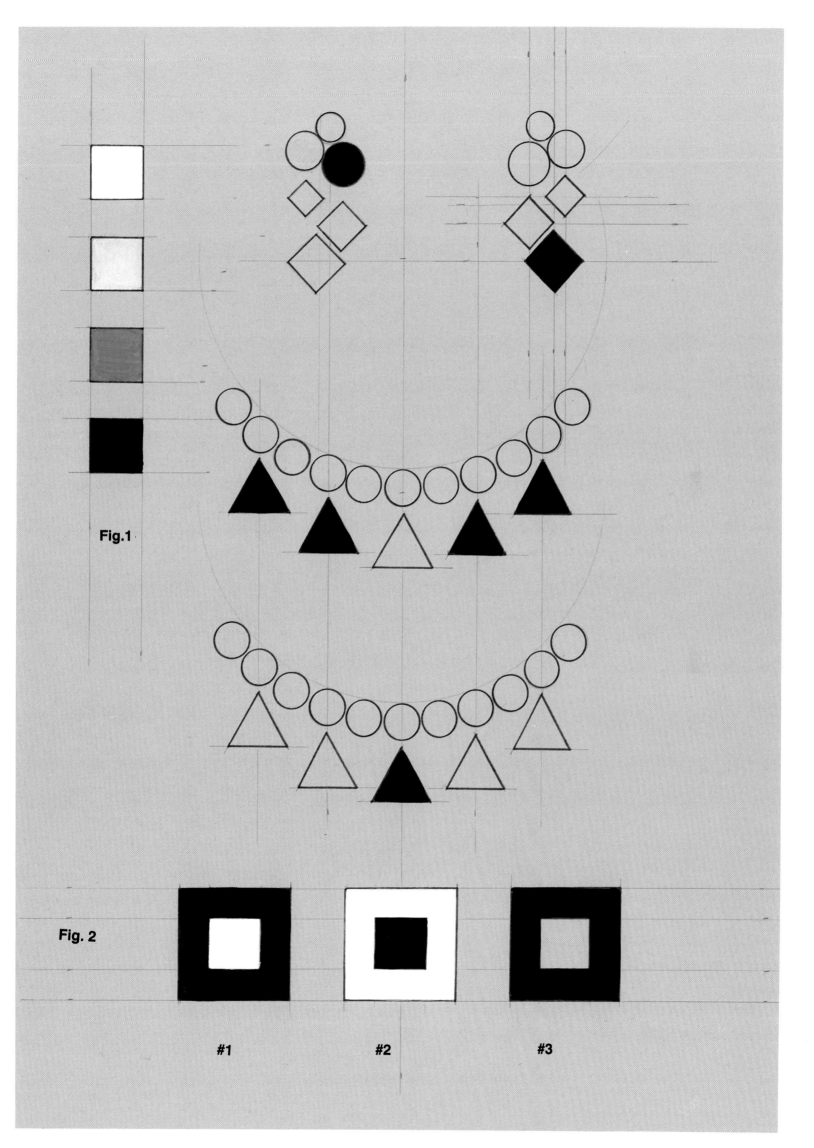

Fig.1

Fig. 2

#1   #2   #3

PLATE 5. STUDY IN ASYMMETRY

At this point we would like to reassure the reader that this page is intended solely as a textbook exercise. Though seemingly complex, once analyzed, the examples in Plate 5 will no longer appear as a bewildering assembly of forms and textures. The necklace is composed of four basic forms: the circle, the triangle, the square and its relative, the rectangle, combined with five textures: light lines, heavy lines, adjacent circles, solid blacks and solid whites.

The balance of this necklace rests upon three factors: the relative sizes of the elements, their placement and overlapping, and their textures. Except for textures, these variables have already been considered in the previous plates.

To maintain the integrity of the various forms, we have avoided massing elements similar in size, shape and texture, spacing the elements so as to obtain a visual equilibrium in the composition. The heavy black borders around some of the circles and the large triangle are used to visually connect and integrate the solid black elements with the lighter textures. Without them, the black forms would seem isolated.

A large form can very well be of a light texture, even solid white in some instances, and keep its full visual weight. This can be seen by the necklace's center triangle, which, though overlapped by smaller and denser shapes, has maintained its identity and strength. The two brooch studies are based on the same principles.

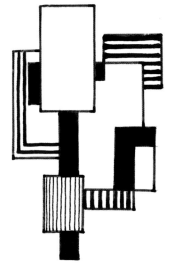

PLATE 6. POSITIVE/NEGATIVE SPACE

Upon looking at any given design, one becomes aware of the positive area, that is, of the elements composing that design. Because the primary attention is focused on the identification of those elements, the surrounding area is not noticed until specifically addressed. This area is called the negative space.

Negative space is best established through contrasting values, and this point is exemplified by the "Swan vs Fish" necklace design in Plate 6. On the left, the black swans are sharply defined in contrast to the white background or negative space. Conversely, the black background on the right allows for the sharp contrast of the fish, while the swans fade away for lack of identifiable negative space.

PLATE 7. POSITIVE/NEGATIVE SPACE II

Plate 7 demonstrates how to increase visual awareness of design by way of negative space and how it can be implemented as a useful tool in jewelry design. In this plate, one side of each design has been delineated with black to emphasize the negative space, while the other side remains on the original gray ground.

The examples illustrated consist of diamond earrings, brooches and a bracelet composed of individually-set stones. In these pieces, the angles at which each stone is placed will determine the silhouette. When working with projects of this nature, it is customary to check the outline, for a single stone misplaced can upset the whole design. This method can be applied to any kind of design, notwithstanding the nature of the elements involved, whether metal or stones, i.e., the floral brooch.

PLATE 8. LIGHT SOURCES: Incidental and Reflected Light

Considering an object in a three-dimensional context, we first study the basic rules of perspective affecting the object: the linear aspect of a shape in a given position in space. To achieve a total transposition of the object from two to three dimensions requires establishing the sense of mass of that form through values dictated by the light source or sources.

Light, in artistic terms, creates various areas of bright and dark values and shadows, and the nuances between values can be infinite in nature. To simplify the study, only five values are used in Plate 8, with white being the highest value.

To gain the maximum effect while minimizing the complexity of multiple light sources, jewelry design is arbitrarily based on a single source of light originating at a 45-degree angle from the top left, as shown by the white "light ray" in the illustration. This simplification will allow for an easier handling of the shading of the design.

Incidental light, which reaches the object in a straight trajectory from its source, is consistent in all these shapes. However, notice in the sphere, cylinder and cone, a light value on the right edge representing the reflected light. All objects of a spherical or curvaceous nature will answer to the same principle of incidental and reflected light. Of no less importance, sharp angles in cubic, pyramidal and angular volumes do not generate a reflected light due to the more abrupt changes of surface angles.

To make a rather technical definition more understandable, the presence of reflected light is due to the reverberation of incidental light from a theoretical background behind the object. That light "bounces back" toward the object, losing in the process part of its original intensity. This is why a reflected light should never be as high in value as the highest incidental light value. Whenever rendering, always remember the source of light because it will allow you to understand and feel the forms and volumes as they should be perceived.

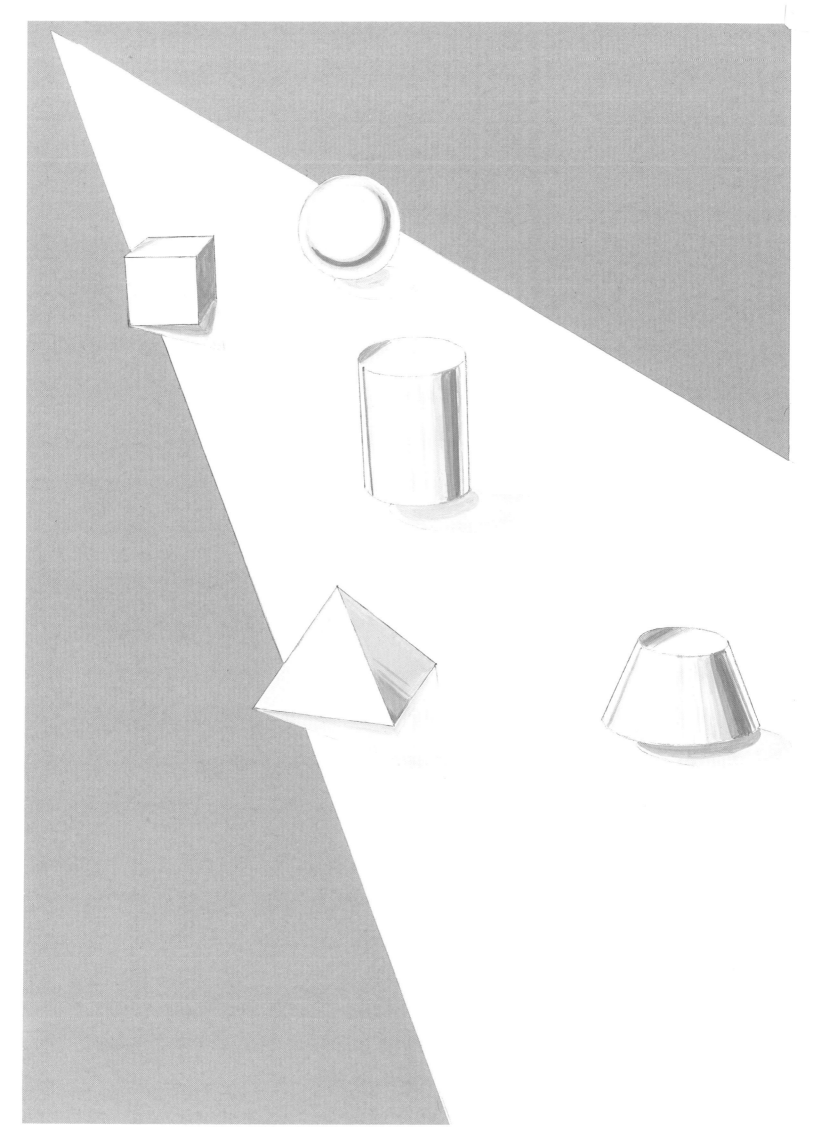

PLATE 9. ELEMENTARY PERSPECTIVE: Volume of Basic Shapes

Perspective, through which we imply the notion of depth, is a broad and interesting subject. Though it cannot be thoroughly studied within the scope of this book, we have chosen to use a few pertinent examples directly connected to jewelry design.

The transition between two-dimensional and three-dimensional form is illustrated here through the use of basic shapes as follows: the square becomes a cube; the rectangle a cylinder, the triangle a four-sided pyramid; the circle a sphere; and the trapezoid an irregular parallelogram.

The appearance of objects in space varies depending upon the angle at which they are viewed. These visual alterations are related to three factors: the eye level or direction, the station point and the vanishing point or points. An object positioned at eye level simply means that the object is perceived by the viewer looking straight forward. The station point is the location from which the viewer is seeing the object. From that station point, as the eye is directed straight forward, a theoretical line can be assumed at the extreme reach of vision. This is the horizon line.

The horizon line must be defined at the very first stage of perspective drawing because it is the line which locates the vanishing point or points. As exemplified in Fig. #1, a cube is viewed in three different perspectives: (a) one vanishing point, (b) two vanishing points, and (c) three vanishing points.

In the last example, vanishing points a and b are located on the horizon line whereas vanishing point c is obtained by extending lines 1, 2 and 3 of the cube downward until they meet at vanishing point c.

Figure #2 illustrates a circular object in perspective. It is inscribed within a square which serves as a guide. The circle, once in perspective, assumes the shape of an ellipse opening more as it is rotated from the center. This perspective is used extensively in drawing rings and bracelets, and will be studied in greater detail with the plates pertaining to those subjects.

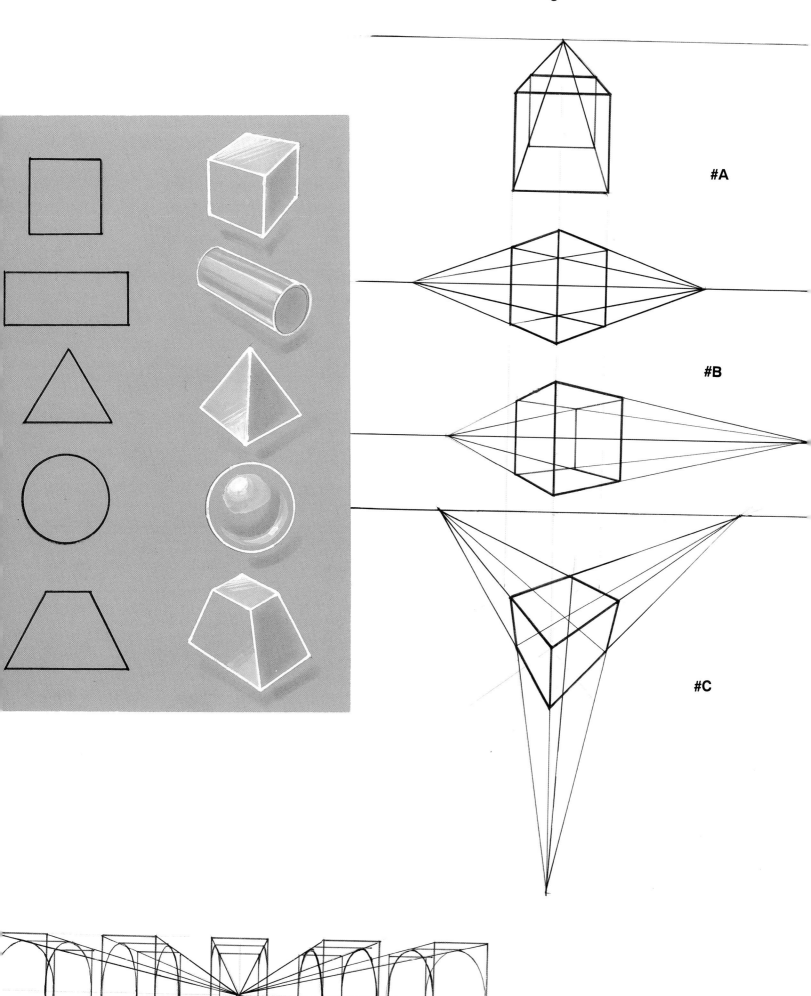

Fig. 1

#A

#B

#C

Fig. 2

PLATE 10. ELEMENTARY PERSPECTIVE (cont'd)

Plate 10 illustrates a cube in three-point perspective seen both from above and below the horizon line. The bottom diagram shows four forms drawn in one-point perspective.

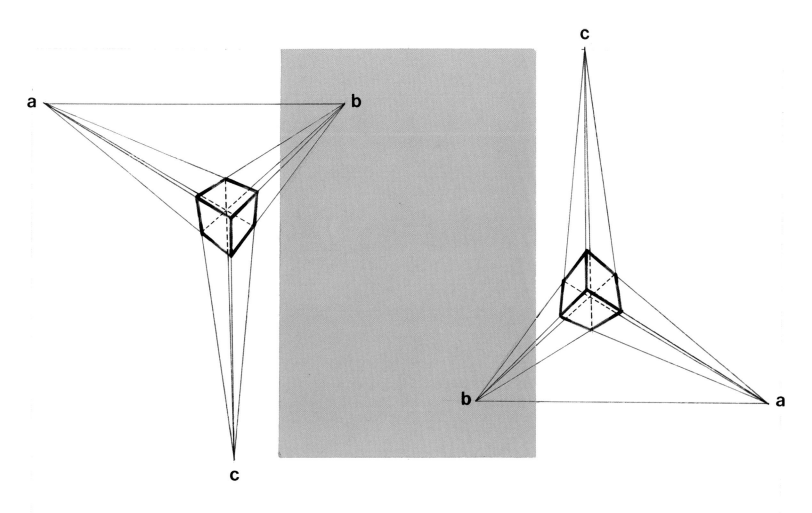
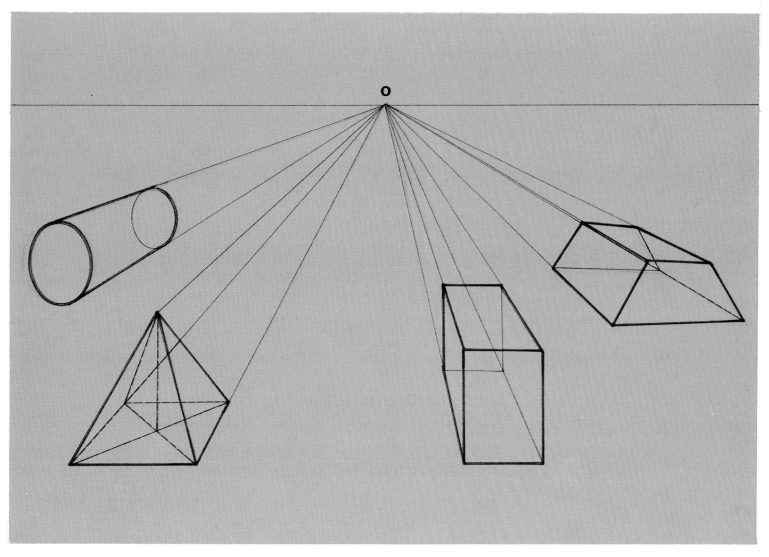

PLATE 11. ELEMENTARY PERSPECTIVE: A Bracelet

This plate illustrates a bracelet reminiscent of the 1940's, of simple forms and contrast conveyed through rounded, convex and angular motives. The elements composing the bracelet have been treated individually to best define their specific perspective.

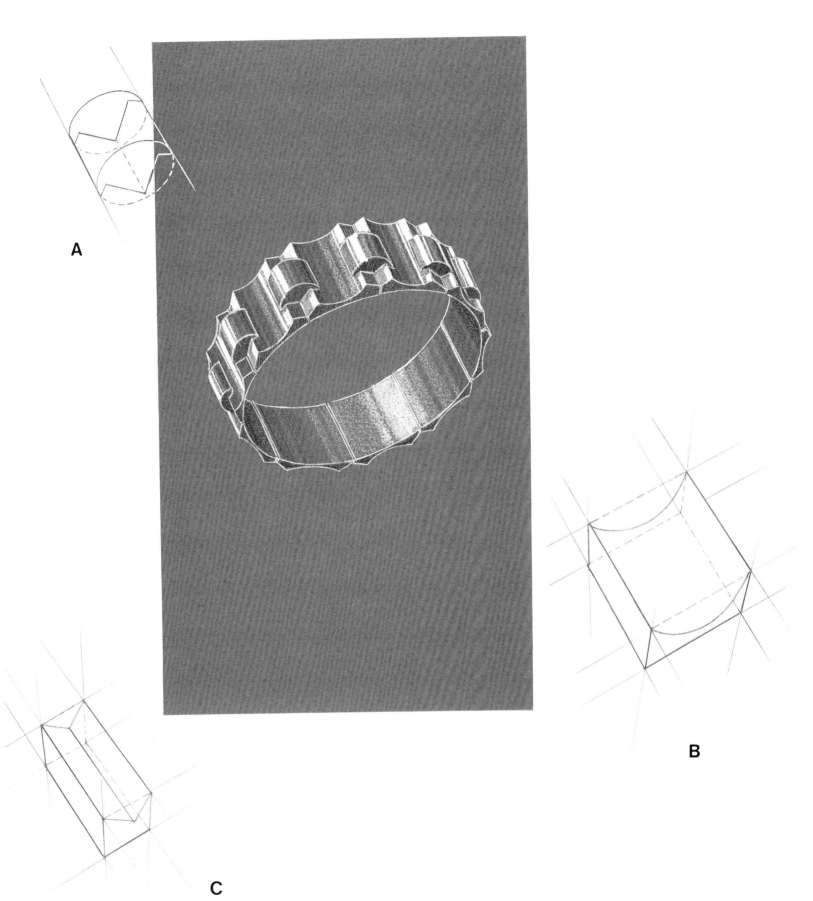

A

B

C

PLATE 12. DOCUMENTARY STUDY: The Flower

       With the documentary study, we are reaching the sources of a designer's creativity. Creativity in our profession can best be described as the ability or the talent to interpret, stylize and combine various elements taken from our natural or man-made environment. A multitude of subjects are available to the "trained" eye of the artist from the animate world to the inanimate.

       We borrowed nature's most delicate creation for our first documentary study: the gladiolus. This study is strictly linear, a pen-and-ink sketch on white bristol paper, meant to highlight the elegance of contours and proportions particular to the flower. A keen sense of observation is applied to such a study, for the eventual reward lies in a faithful reproduction. No interpretation on the part of the artist is needed at this stage.

       We advise our students to start the documentary study with a light pencil sketch in order to get familiar with the subject. A satisfactory pencil sketch should be obtained before proceeding to the pen and ink sketch. Working in pen and ink will help develop a sense for linear shapes and rhythms in addition to the discipline required for a "clean" rendering technique. Each curve, each line has its importance and it is the way in which they are combined that will determine the success of the study.

PLATE 13. DOCUMENTARY STUDY: The Flower. Detail Study

To further the documentation of the gladiolus, the various components of the flower should be examined. Plate 13 illustrates five drawings detailing the leaves, buds, and geometrical pattern of the petal, as well as two views of the whole flower.

The choice of paper and media used is very important. In this plate, a medium gray "canson" paper was used, being compatible with black and white pencils. The slight texture of this paper is more receptive to pencils than a smoother paper.

The color choice of paper has a definite purpose, which is to render volume using the gray of the paper as the medium value and black and white pencils for high and low values.

PLATE 14. DOCUMENTARY STUDY: The Flower - Application to Jewelry

   Moving from the documentary study to jewelry design, Plate 14 illustrates seven creations inspired by the gladiolus. The brooches and earrings are sketched in black and white pencil on gray paper, as in Plate 13, and further emphasizes the practical aspect of primary sketches. These designs could be interpreted in a broad variety of materials including gold, diamonds, colored stones, or even silver.

   Three brooch designs (Fig. #'s 1, 2, 3) feature both floral and foliate motifs in elongated patterns, and two are button-like designs based on the flower.

   The earrings follow identical treatments: Earring #4 is definitely "on the ear" and circular, and Earring #5 uses a "dropping" leaf to elongate the shape downward past the ear-lobe.

#4

#1

#5

#2

#3

PLATE 15. THE FLOWER SET (Color Roughs)

Plate 15, although anticipated from a rendering point of view, demonstrates the way in which three sketches become closely related stylewise in what we professionally call a "set." The use of identical elements of design, not forcibly in size, but rather in the way they are stylized, is what ties these pieces together. The petals, creased in a similar manner and held together by a roundish tie-over, and the larger leaf shapes forming the body of both bracelet and necklace, indeed belong to the same "set." This "set" adequately illustrates the principles involved in what is sometimes coined a "family" look.

PLATE 16. DOCUMENTARY STUDY: The Sea Anemone

From the earthly surroundings of the gladiolus to the watery world of our next subject, the following documentary study will now turn to yet another specimen of delicate beauty and elegance in motion: the sea anemone.

The three studies in Plate 16 reveal the fluid lines so typical of this sea "flower." Undulating slowly in the water currents, it becomes an ever graceful silhouette of the underwater scenery.

The studies at the bottom of the plate examine the details of the individual filaments, their particular shape and the way in which they connect to the center of the anemone. Although this "flower" belongs to the animal world, its resemblance to vegetal species is such that it is more like a "living flower." The name originated from the ancient Greeks, who called it Anemone, "The Daughter of the Wind."

PLATE 17. DOCUMENTARY STUDY: The Sea Anemone (Application to Jewelry)

The study in Plate 17 shows how the graceful curves of the anemone's filaments lend themselves to many interpretations based on the use of tapered gold wires.

Earring #1 is built around a stylized center from which wire elements flow in a fan-like shape. This look is meant to reflect a certain bulk, whereas in Earring #2, the feeling is of a more fluid nature following the contour of the lobe in an upward thrust. The absence of a central motif helps the dynamic of the design, the eye following the curve of the wires.

Brooch #3 is based on the same principle as Earring #1, where the central element of pearl and diamonds becomes the focal point, contrasting with the lighter surrounding wires.

The other two brooches relate to Earring #2. Without a definite center, the elements harmonize into a flowing shape reminiscent of the real anemone.

#1

#3

#2

PLATE 18. THE SEA ANEMONE SET

The sea anemone set in Plate 18 also relies on the use of finely tapered gold wires to create the feeling of fluidity. The bud-like elements, meant to add visual strength to the wire work, also gives mechanical strength and allows the jeweler to adequately link the various components of the necklace and bracelet. This type of awareness must be ever present in sound design, which must be both aesthetically and mechanically relevant.

PLATE 19. DOCUMENTARY STUDY: The Sea Shell

       With Plate 19, we further explore some of Neptune's hidden treasures, one of Nature's most tailored creations: the sea shell.

       Sea shells offer a vast field for useful documentation. From time immemorial, they have captured the eye of artists for their endless diversity, graceful proportions, intricate textures and striking dynamic forms. Indeed, some of the very first body ornaments were artistically contrasting sea shells stringed into necklaces and bracelets.

       This black and white pencil study on gray paper explores forms, textures and the repartition of "color" as featured in the two bottom shells.

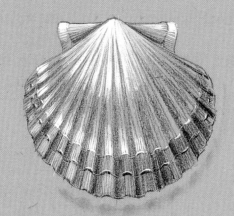

PLATE 20. DOCUMENTARY STUDY: The Sea Shell (Application to Jewelry)

The five pencil studies in Plate 20 demonstrate the adaptability of the sea shell to jewelry. Staying close to nature, Brooch #1 creates a pinwheel pattern and the contrast and visual interest is determined by the convex or concave volume of each shell.

Earring #2 adds diversification through the use of textures, and Earring # 3 uses different shell shapes to form a pendant.

Departing from a literal interpretation, Earring #4 is more stylized and the use of wires or "fluting" becomes a texture in itself. Brooch #5, which is basically similar, elegantly links two elements.

#1

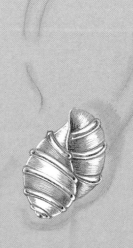

#2

#4

#3

#5

PLATE 21. DOCUMENTARY STUDY: The Sea Shell Necklace

       The necklaces in Plate 21 are two interpretations using a repeated motif. In Necklace #1, the use of the fluted shells placed at contrasting angles creates a rhythmic pattern. Necklace #2 is composed of closely fitting shells, the volume of the shell being the major element of interest in creating a flowing pattern.

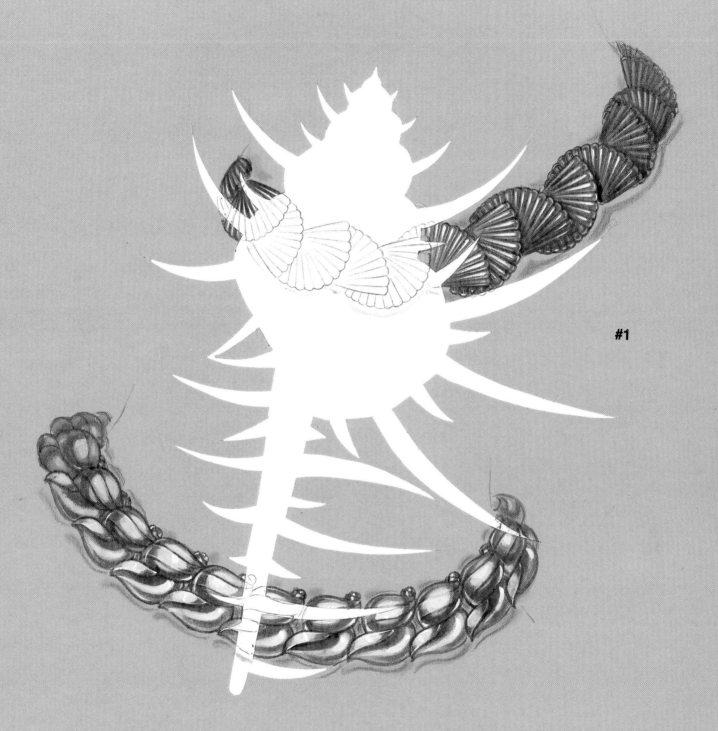

#1

#2

PLATE 22. DOCUMENTARY STUDY: The Ribbon

No study would be complete without the ribbon and its basic use, the bow. One could surmise that, as early ingenuity devised the use of strings and ribbons as a means of securing garments, it was only a matter of time before the bow became a type of jewel.

The graceful folds of bows can vary to a great extent without ever losing the supple quality which has made them the favorite subject of countless creations.

Study #1 is meant to familiarize the student with a pencil rendering of values in a curling ribbon without any folds. Relative to the light source, the values graduate from light to dark in a progressive pattern. The reflected light, indicated by a light value, is used to soften and accentuate the curve at the right edge of the ribbon.

Studies #2 and #3 both show pleats typical of the bow and use a fairly wide ribbon in order to obtain a maximum of folds conditioned by the tightness of the knot.

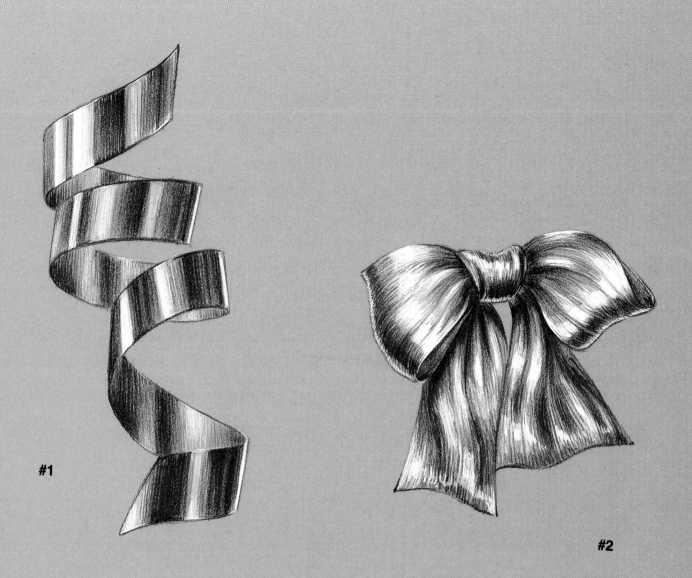

#1

#2

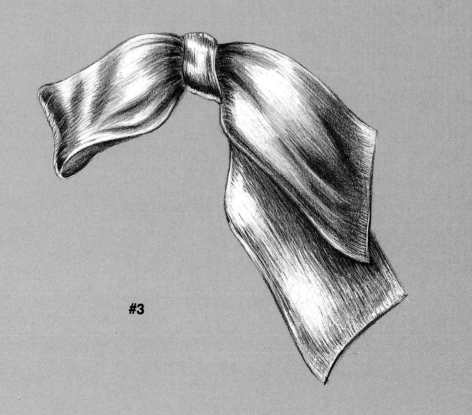

#3

PLATE 23. DOCUMENTARY STUDY: The Ribbon (Application to Jewelry)

The versatility of the ribbon is demonstrated here through five designs featuring a wide ribbon and a narrow one.

Earring #1 links the narrow ribbon to a curved heart-shape, creating an open volume as well as a sizeable earring. The absence of pleats preserves the integrity of the shape.

Brooch #2 evokes a tailored look derived from the simplicity of a wide ribbon tied in a loose knot.

Brooch #3 is a substantial bow which relies on the movement, folds and billowy surfaces of ribbons.

Brooch #4 is formed by a tapering pattern of overlapping narrow ribbons, creating a rhythmic effect. The ribbons, as in the earring, are devoid of folds in order not to distract the eye from the continuous flow of lines.

Ring #5, simple yet effective, is made of a single bow crossing the finger. The center knot is smooth and contrasts with the folds on its sides, lending strength to the center of the ring.

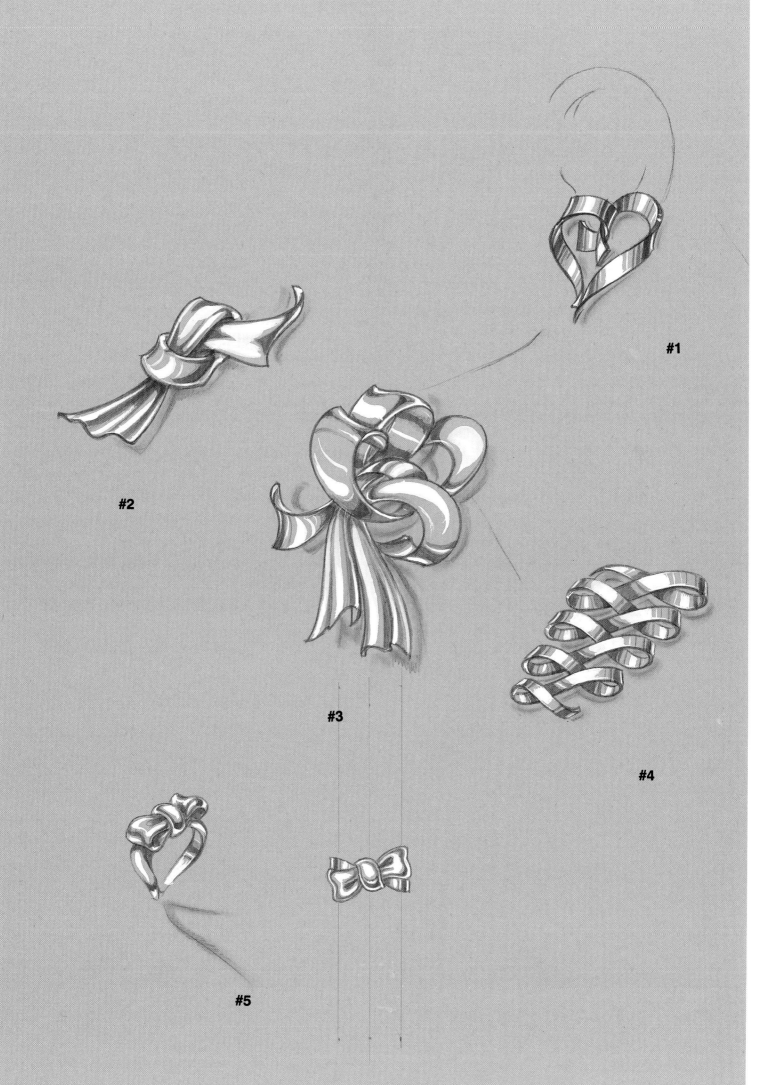

#1

#2

#3

#4

#5

#5

PLATE 24. DOCUMENTARY STUDY: The Ribbon (Cont'd)

Exploring further the use of the ribbon we introduce a three- piece set: necklace, earrings and bracelet, examples #1, #2, and #3. Fully rendered in yellow gold, they are based on similar identifiable movements, more specifically the way in which the ribbon forms a double knot at the center of each jewel. Technically, the necklace and bracelet would be semi-flexible, the ribbon elements flexing at their overlapping points.

Brooch #4 takes advantage of an undulating effect in the loops of the bow, contrasting with the smoothly pleated ends falling from the knot.

Brooch #5 joins contrasting movement with a certain looseness, the absence of a tight knot at its center allowing the ends to curve gently downward.

Bracelet #6 combines a tight weave with a more relaxed knot. The flexibility here is obtained through the links formed by the weaving ribbon.

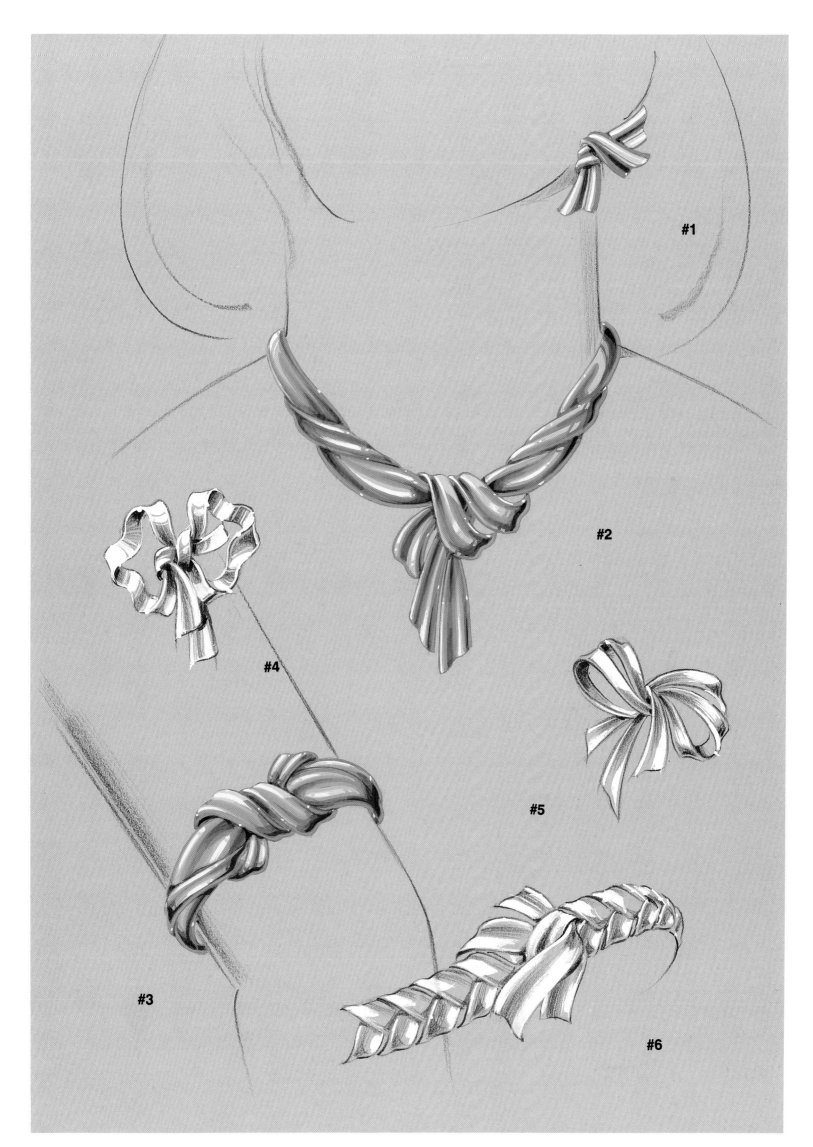

#1

#2

#3

#4

#5

#6

Part II
Metal and Stone Rendering Techniques

PLATE 25. GOLD: Basic Palette. Gouaches & Watercolors

Successful gold rendering depends on the choice of appropriate colors. A succinct study of gold painting techniques through the works of fine arts masters reveals a great variety of approaches to possible color schemes.

Since polished metal surfaces reflect surrounding forms and colors within their angle of refraction, one must introduce a certain amount of subjectivity, in the use of colors, in order not to detract from the rendering.

Plate 25 indicates the six colors required for the gold palette. The colors are specific manufacturer's brand names for the colors we recommend, and are listed in the "Basic Tools" description (Plate 1).

The first color, applied as a medium value base, is Monaco Yellow. The second color, the first low value, is a Light Brown, followed by the third color and the deepest low value, a Van Dyke Brown. Leaving the low values and entering the high values, a Golden Yellow used with an additional touch of white gouache is the first high value, followed by a Cadmium Primrose. This yellow should also be mixed with white to reach the intended tone. However, the consistency of the final tone must not be weakened through an excess of water. We recommend Pelikan Graphic White as the white, which is ready to be used with a minimal addition of water. Incidentally, it is the same gouache recommended for diamond rendering for its strength and luminosity.

The last color indicated on the plate is Cadmium Yellow Deep, exclusively used for rendering reflected light.

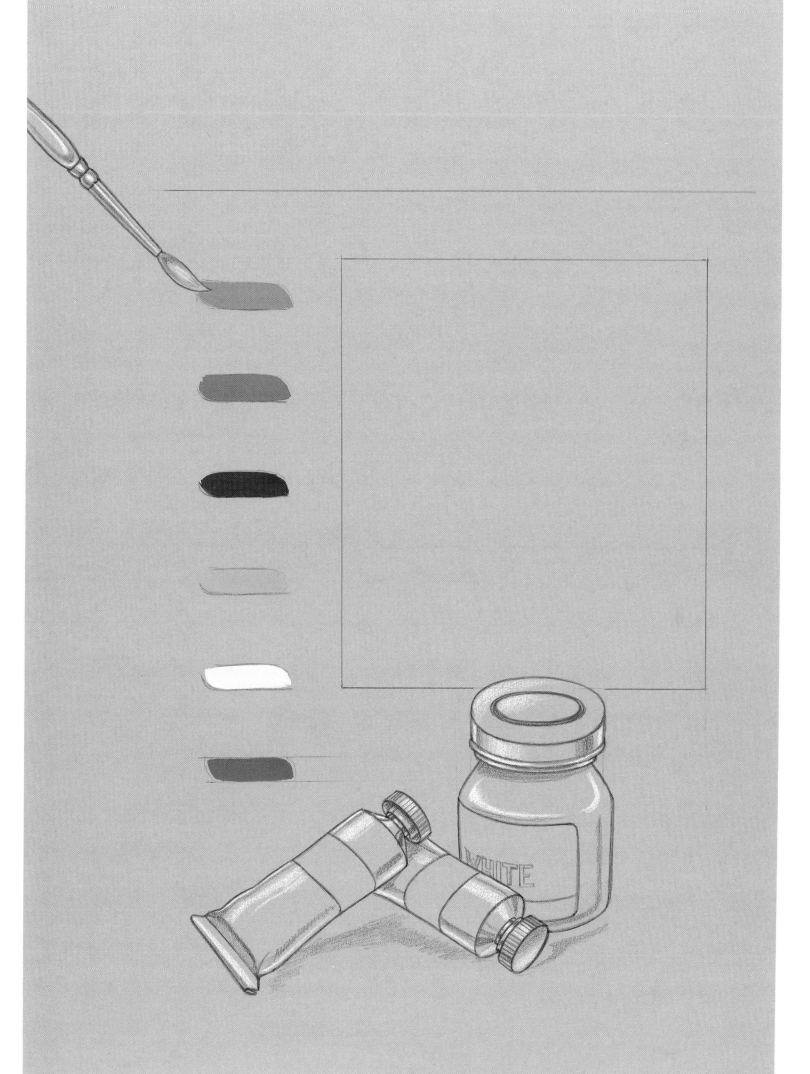

Plate 26. EXAMPLE: The Ribbon

Having previously studied ribbons in our black-and-white sketches will facilitate the approach to fully colored rendering. Again, as a rule, we would strongly advise students to first establish a value scheme compatible with their subject in this black-and-white approach before attempting color rendering.

Plate 26 demonstrates the working of color values in four steps:

Step # 1: Apply the medium value Monaco Yellow to the whole surface of the design. It is essential to let the gouache dry thoroughly before working over the area for very specific reasons. First, applying a second "wash" while the first one is still wet will result in an uncontrolled mixing of tones, the "bottom" wash absorbing partially the "top" one. Second, the bleeding resulting from that accidental mixing will cancel the precision of the brushwork which is ever so important in rendering metallic surfaces.

Step # 2: Working in the low values, Light Brown and Van Dyke Brown, which are both used somewhat diluted, we first apply the Light Brown, then the Van Dyke Brown for the areas requiring the deepest low values.

Step # 3: Introducing the first light value with Golden Yellow, we apply it in the areas where incidental light reaches the surface.

Step # 4: Giving a final touch to the rendering, we apply the second light value, Cadmium Primrose mixed with white, in the areas with the highest exposure to the incidental light. One more step is needed to complete our rendering: applying the reflected light Cadmium Yellow Deep on the edges of the curling ribbon.

At this point the rendering is technically complete. However, you might wish to dramatize a particular element with a touch of Van Dyke Brown or Cadmium Primrose and white. But be careful with the highest and lowest values in the color scheme. They can make or break your rendering. The low value used with exaggeration will darken the gold beyond recognition, while an overdose of high value will result in a pasty surface devoid of brilliancy.

Observe the brushwork in the two bows, the ways in which the values have been used to bring out specific volumes. Remember, the brush strokes must always emphasize the form they are creating. As with the ribbon, the vertical lines accent the flat nature of the surface and the look of highly polished metal. The width of the value areas are also varied in order to avoid a "flag-like" feeling.

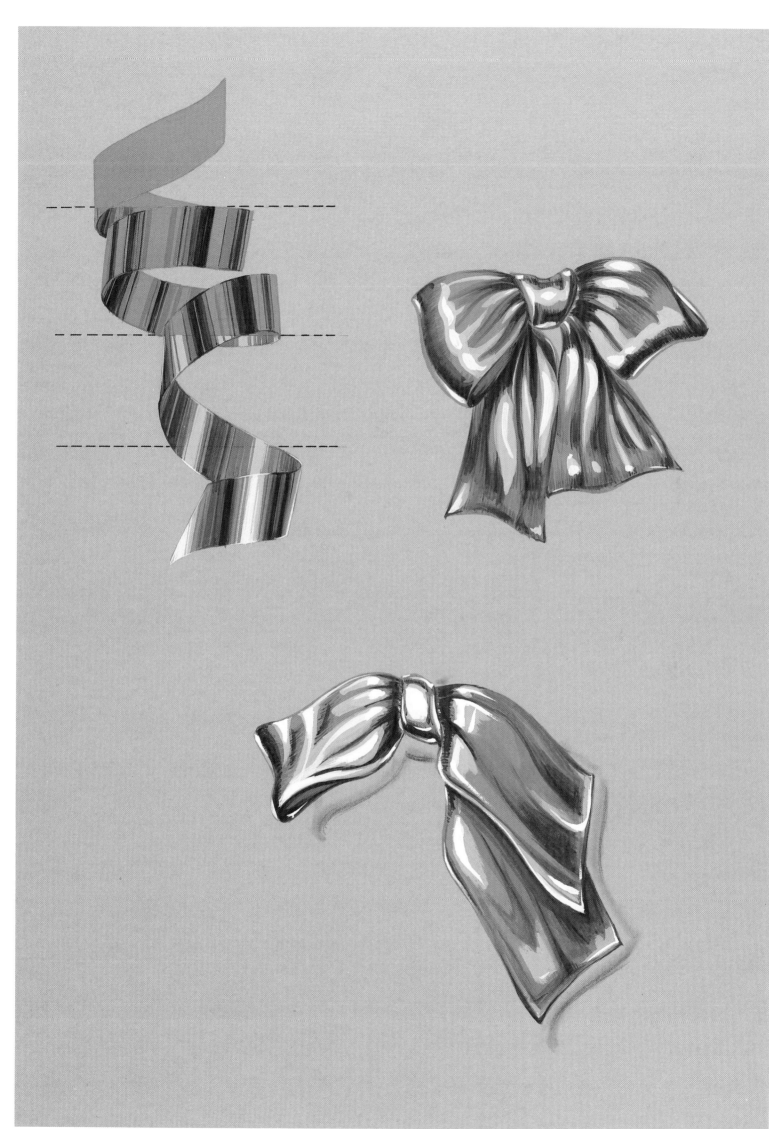

PLATE 27. EXAMPLE: Metal Strips

The gold rendering technique is further explored in Plate 27 with metal strips shaped in various fashions, twisted, pinched, domed, angular, concave and convex configurations. These models serve to demonstrate how the brushwork accentuates the nature of the surface.

In the sharply folded strips, the values are best controlled by short strokes worked width-wise, whereas in the concave, twisted and pinched models, a length-wise stroke will allow a maximum of control.

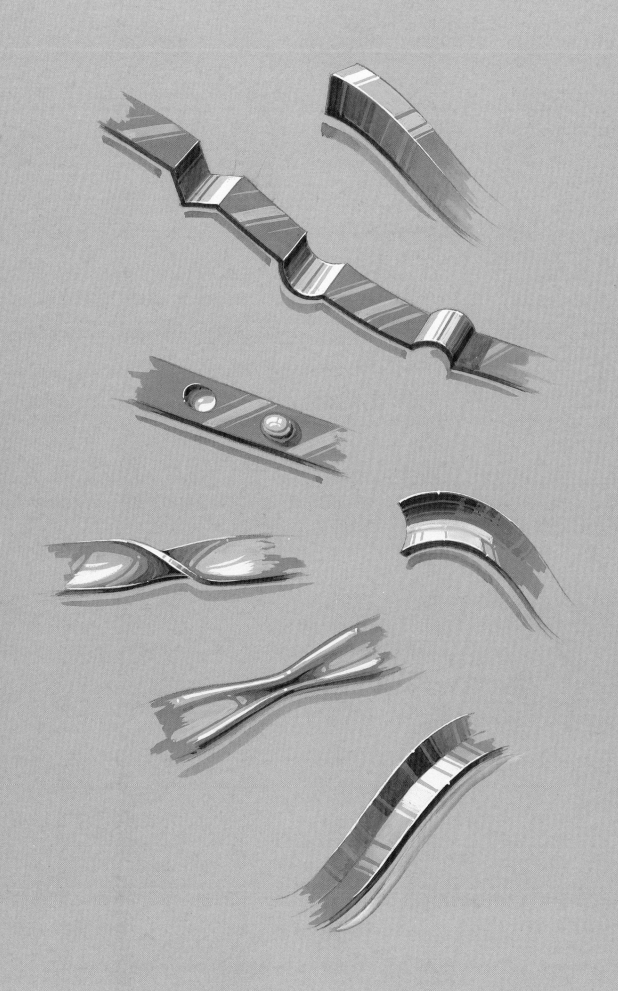

PLATE 28. EXAMPLE: The Wire

Widely used in jewelry, gold wires can assume a great variety of forms, textures and, of course, diameters. The six gold wires in Plate 28 exemplify the types most often encountered: a round wire, a loosely twisted double wire, a tightly twisted double wire, a bead wire, a single twisted wire, and lastly, a tapered round wire. The brooch illustrated purposely makes use of the six types of wires featured.

Round and square wires far from complete the wire types available. Drawing plates provide the jeweler with a very diversified assortment, including oval, rectangle, olive-shape, triangle, heart-shape and star-shape. Each type can further differ by a highly polished, matte, brushed or textured finish.

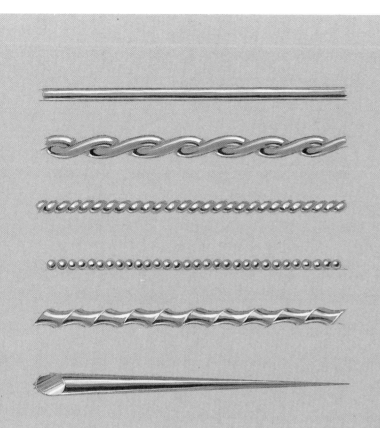

PLATE 29. EXAMPLE: The Textures

From the earliest goldsmithing attempts to the present, jewelers have understood the malleability of precious metals. As a result, they have engraved, hammered, beaded, chased and shaped gold and silver into an impressive array of textures. Although the lost wax method was known at an early stage, it is with the recent addition of the hard carving waxes that the variety in textures has increased a hundred-fold. In Plate 29, we have chosen a simple, leaf-like brooch to be our vehicle in the nine examples illustrating textures most often used.

In all the examples, a common approach to these different textures consists in rendering the volume prior to applying the texture. Our advice concerning this first stage of rendering is to soften the contrast of values so as to avoid a highly polished effect at the outset, in order to preserve the choice of finish on the ensuing texture.

1. Brushed Texture. Very fine, parallel lines have been painted over the initial values, covering the entire surface. The effect of these lines, which serve to simulate brushed gold, automatically dull the surface, and the feeling is one of half-tones, soft and matte.

2. Engraved Texture. This example is also treated in a linear fashion: the lines, more widely spaced, are engraved suggesting the veins of the leaf. Since the surface has been only partially textured, a brighter finish is apparent in this leaf.

3. Hammered Texture. This technique consists in simulating the hammer strokes by painting depressions or concave marks at close intervals. This texture also dulls the surface.

4. Florentine Texture. This texture, bearing the name of the city from which it originated, is characterized by very fine lines engraved in a variety of cross-hatched patterns. Here again, the look is soft and matte.

5. Scale Texture. This technique can be achieved either by chasing the metal or carving wax. This example reflects contrasting values that have been added to render a highly polished surface. Achieving a matte finish would entail covering the entire surface with fine lines as in the first brushed texture example.

6. Splintery Texture. For a lack of a more identifiable term, this texture is also chased or carved and can be rendered in a dull or polished finish, as in the example.

7. Basket Weave Textures. Rendered either in a matte or polished finish, the depth of the weave requires the use of well-defined contrasting values. This texture can also be chased or carved.

8. Baton Texture. This alternative texture is rendered interesting by combining polished and matte finishes, where only the stick-like elements are polished.

9. Beaded Texture. This texture, a type of granulation, concludes our excursion into the field of textured surfaces, which, in reality, can be as varied as creativity and technical knowledge.

PLATE 30. GOLD: Alternative Technique (Ink and Gouache)

Demonstrated in five successive steps, this ink gouache technique starts with a clean line drawing of the leaf in a brown colored pencil. At this early stage, dark values are indicated in pencil along the twisting areas.

The second step consists in the application of a waterproof sepia ink over the line drawing. Going over the dark value areas will require the thinning of the ink with a touch of water in order to maintain the value gradations.

Step Three involves applying a thin wash of white over the entire surface of the leaf. At this point, let us remind our student of the ever important need to let the ink or gouache dry thoroughly between each step.

Step Four is the addition of high values in a thicker white in the proper areas.

Step Five, the last and final step, consists of the application of waterproof yellow ink over the whole surface. The brush should not be overloaded with ink and the brushwork should be light and precise. If the first glaze does not cover in a satisfactory manner, let the glaze dry thoroughly and then apply a second glaze. This recommendation is made with the specific intention to spare our student the somewhat agonizing experience of "bleeding" layers of gouache washed out by an excess of ink.

Serious practice is the key to successful rendering, and once the ink-gouache rendering technique is assimilated, it will offer a time-saving advantage. Another positive aspect of this type of rendering is the pleasing transparency particular to most glazing techniques, which we will further explore in the chapter on stone rendering.

PLATE 31. WHITE METAL: Basic Palette. Gouache and Watercolor

       As with the gold palette, white metal requires a range of tones suited to its appearance. Plate 31 indicates the five values from white to black used in rendering white metal.

       The palette is as follows, from the highest to the lowest value, white to black: the first high value is Pelikan Graphic White alone; the subsequent three values are a combination of the same white with increasing proportions of Neutral Tint. We want to specify that, although the neutral tint belongs to the watercolor pigment family and therefore is a transparent color, it blends easily when mixed with white gouache. Lastly, the lowest value is Jet Black.

       The medium value, the third tone indicated on the diagram, is the base upon which the lower and higher values are established to create the volume.

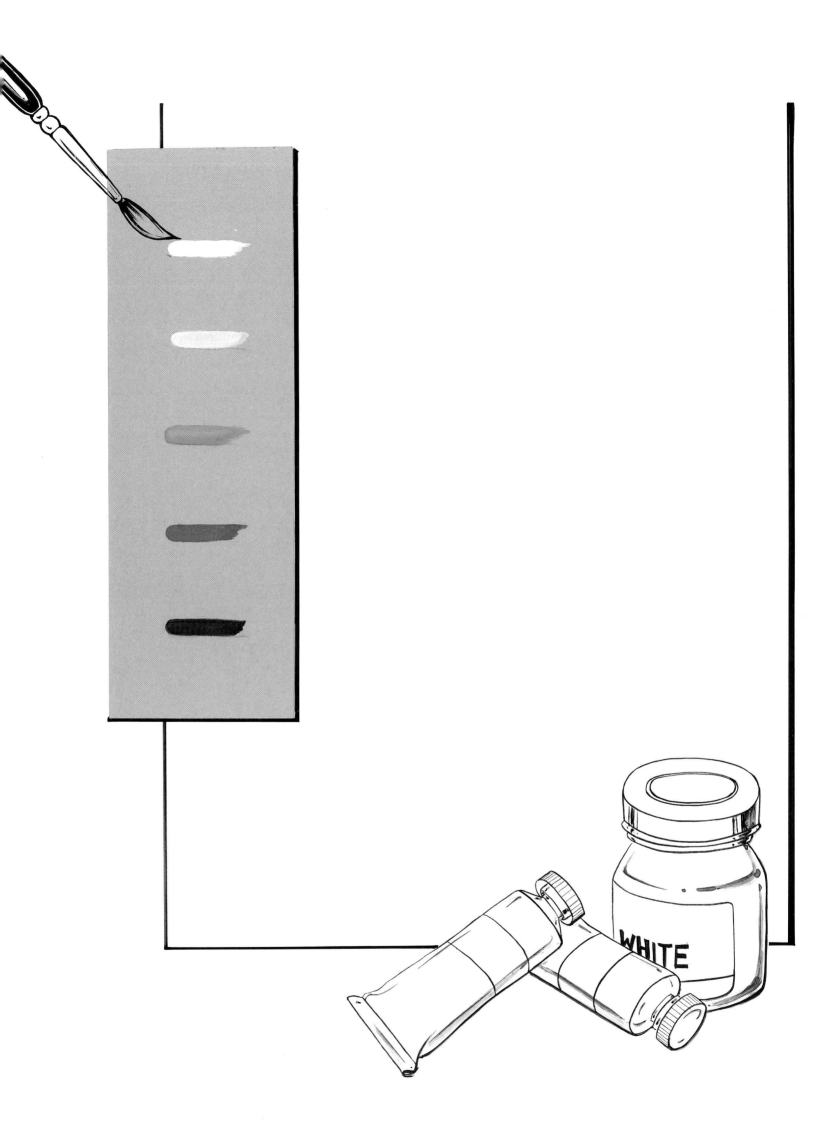

PLATE 32. SILVER AND GOLD

Plate 32 consists of two necklaces and a bracelet which combine gold and silver. Although the three pieces could have been interpreted either in all-gold or all-silver, the purpose was to use both metals to show how, even with varying color schemes, the values within each scheme are identical in nature and intent.

Since the rendering technique of white metal is comparable to that of gold, refer to our detailed explanation of the process with reference to Plates 25 through 29.

Remember, the excessive use of the darkest or lightest values could ruin the intended result. "What was true for the goose is true for the gander" is indeed valid for white metal rendering. Notwithstanding the metal, a crisp and "sparkling" rendering depends ultimately on identical principles.

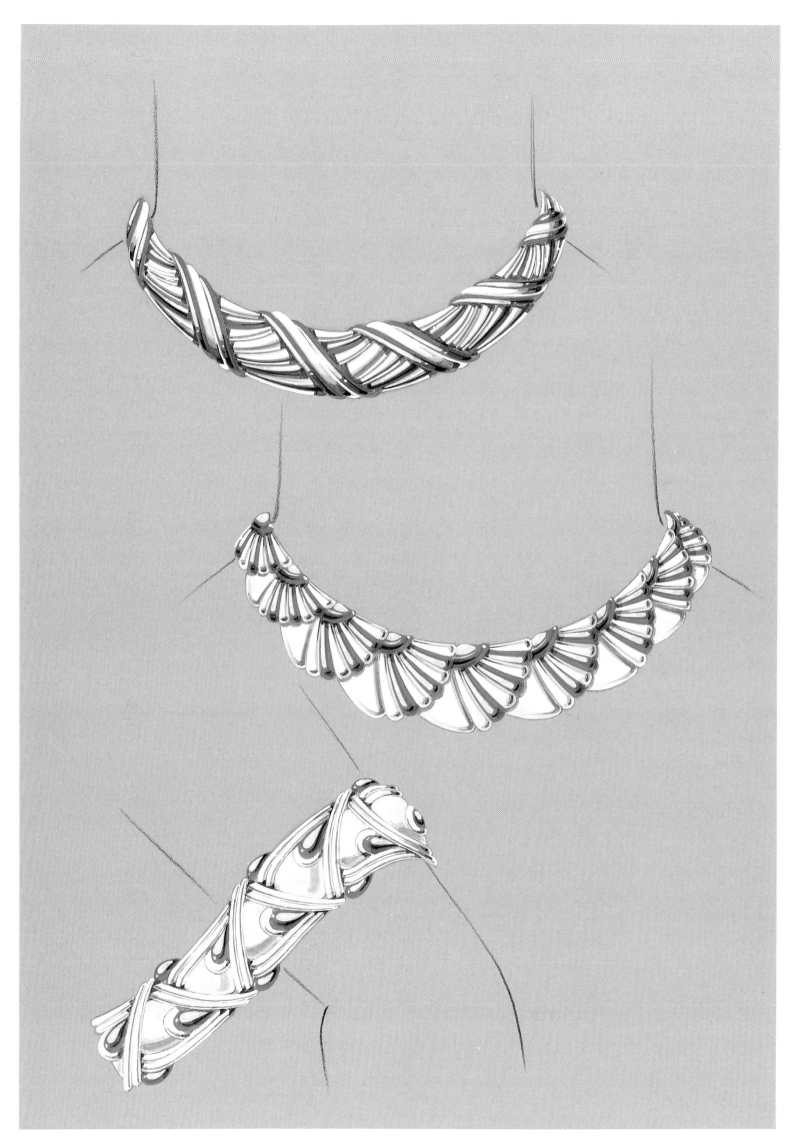

PLATE 33. RENDERING DIAMONDS: Shapes, Cuts and Faceting

Without a doubt the most well known among gemstones, diamonds have been valued for their intrinsic beauty and enhancing quality whenever used in connection with colored gems. To a jewelry designer, the ability to render diamonds well is a basic requirement. Professionally, whenever considering a client's reaction to a design presentation, the excitement needed to positively motivate the prospective buyer depends crucially on the rendering technique of the artist. We have always felt that an interesting idea should not be betrayed by a lack of rendering ability.

Let us examine the subject at hand; the diamond. Plate 33 is divided into two parts: on the left is a top-view line study of the faceting of each diamond shape. These shapes are known as follows: a round brilliant cut, a pear-shape, a marquise or navette, a heart-shape, a scissor-cut and an emerald-cut, an oval ceylon-cut, a briolette in the shape of a faceted tear-drop, a triangular stone, and two baguettes, one straight and one tapered (enlarged for clarity).

The above-mentioned shapes are the most commonly used. However, being mindful of the constant experimentation in the diamond-cutting industry, we would advise our student to keep abreast with trade magazines for any new diamond shapes or cuts.

Stone sizes can vary to a great extent. The Gemological Institute of America (G.I.A.) publishes comparative tables of diamond sizes, weights and shapes. These tables represent an adequate source of information for the designer.

The primary purpose of Plate 33 is to familiarize the student with diamonds and their faceting. Once this is understood, the step-by-step rendering will be considerably simplified.

Round Brilliant Cut

 Pear Shape

 Marquise or Navette

 Heart Shape

 Scissor-cut

 Emerald-cut

 Ceylon-cut

 Briolette

 Triangle-cut

  Baguettes (Straight & Tapered)

PLATES 34 AND 35. THE DIAMOND: Round, Pear and Marquise Shape

Plate 34 illustrates the rendering process of round, marquise and pear-shape diamonds in six distinct steps. Each step adds to the preceding one from left to right until it is completed at the bottom in each example.

Step #1: After tracing the outline in a white line (gouache), apply an initial "wash" of white over the entire surface of the stone (Note: This "wash" should be diluted with enough water to obtain a gray value). This is the base upon which to build up successive values. Again, let washes dry thoroughly between each step.

Step #2: Apply a second wash, slightly higher in value, splitting the stone in two areas with the lighter area on the right. With the constant source of incidental light at 11 o'clock, we are already implying the depth of the stone's pavilion at this stage of the rendering.

Step #3: We are now ready for the faceting. Following the diagram in Plate 33, the facets are traced in a fine white line. Let us point out the importance of the brushwork in relation to the thickness of the "faceting." The sharp, neat and incisive look of the facets depends entirely on crisp structural lines.

Step #4: For the third value we fill in the areas of the stone exposed to direct incidental light. These are the three facets (or star facets) connected to the table on the upper left; the pavilion facets converging to the center of the table and the crown facets located to the far right of the stone. Although not directly exposed to incidental light, these last facets are rendered in high values because of a refraction factor somewhat similar to the "reflected light."

Step #5: Using a higher white value, we brighten the facet of the pavilion directly in line with the incidental light, and also the small "reflected light" facets along the right edge of the girdle.

Step #6: The final step is to go over the star facet in the upper left side of the crown with pure white. The rendering is now complete, offering both the volume and brilliancy of diamonds.

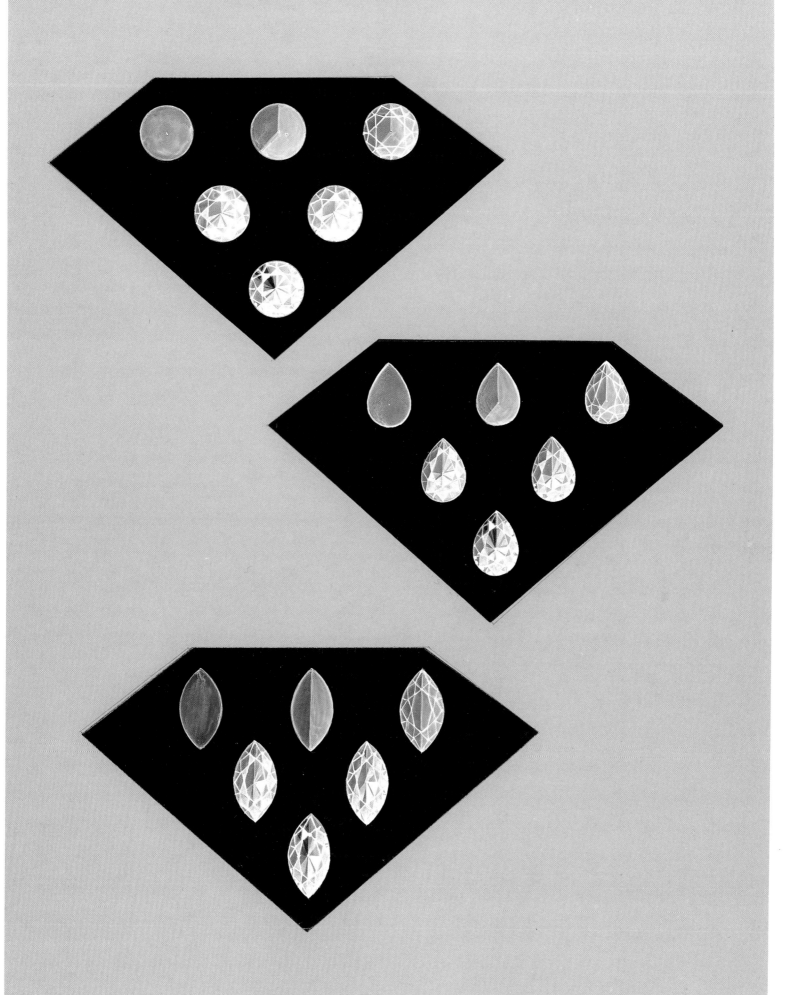

PLATE 35. THE DIAMOND: Emerald, Oval and Briolette Cut

      This technique is applicable to all diamonds shown in Plates 33, 34 and 35. Note that two stones, the emerald cut and the briolet, present a slight variation in their faceting. The emerald cut requires long, straight facets on its crown, as well as part of the pavilion, where six triangular facets are present at the angles. The long facets on the right side of the stone are broken into segments to imply the sparkle of the reflected light. The briolet takes on the shape of a drop, and the facets are all of a diamond shape, criss-crossing the surface of the stone.

      An attentive study of each illustrated step will benefit our students in their efforts to master this rendering process.

      The colored stones are closely related to the diamond, and having practiced diamond rendering, our next step in the realm of precious colored stones will appear quite familiar.

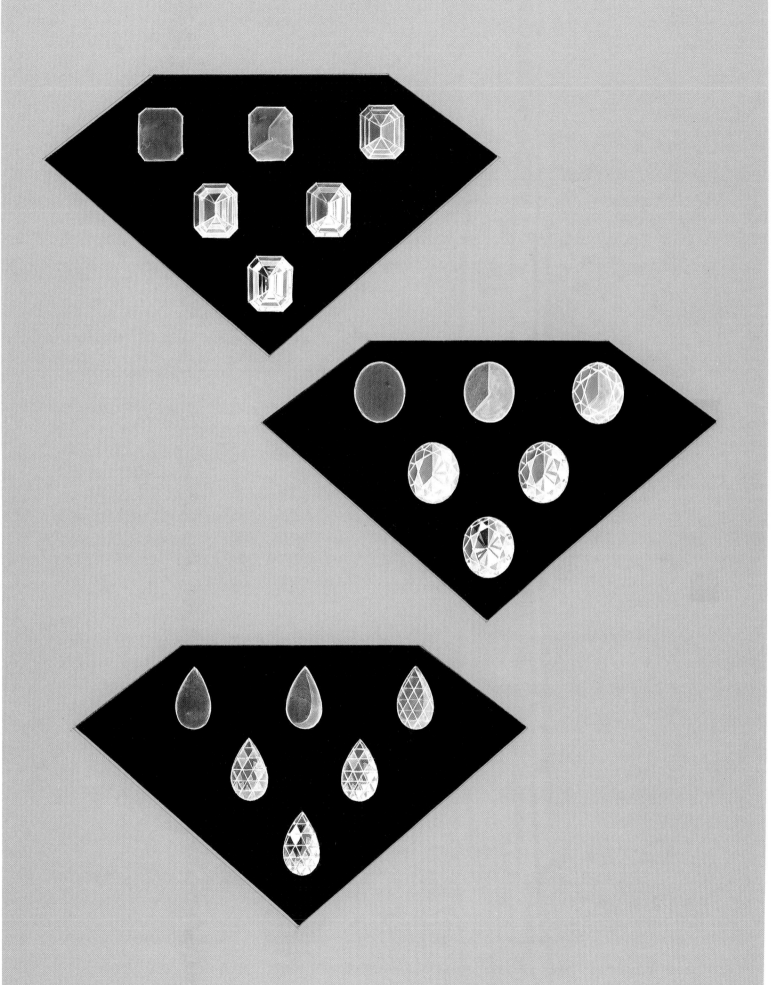

PLATE 36, 37 AND 38. PRECIOUS COLORED GEMSTONES: Sapphire, Ruby and Emerald (Shapes, Cuts and Faceting)

Precious colored gemstones fall into two identifiable categories, faceted stones and cabochons. We are already familiar with the faceted stone through our study of diamonds. Stones such as sapphires, rubies and emeralds are mostly cut along the same guidelines as diamonds, relative to their specific shapes. On the other hand, the cabochon does not include faceting, its overall shape being a smooth domed round or oval shape, or a cushion-like square or triangle.

Plate 36 indicates the full rendering of an oval faceted sapphire in five steps:

Step #1: A wash of the stone's color, blue in this case, is applied to the entire surface. Since the color transparency achieved through the "glazing" technique depends on the use of transparent pigments, we will be using watercolors throughout this process. Opaque colors mixed with white gouache would cancel the depth and brilliancy of the rendering.

Step #2: The second step involves the line faceting in white gouache. Note that the initial blue wash should be dry.

Step #3: Step 3 consists of applying the light values, incidental and reflected. The white gouache should be sufficiently consistent, avoiding an excess of water, which would result in the bleeding of the wash and loss of facet definition. If the value obtained is not adequate, let the surface dry and go back with another wash until the value builds up to the right intensity.

Step #4: The glazing, technically the most demanding, involves applying a wash of blue over the stone as lightly as possible. An excess of water will blur the facet's lines, and conversely, a lack of water will blend the white gouache into the color background.

To avoid such problems, we recommend our student apply a few strokes of white gouache on a separate sheet of black paper and use these areas as "testing grounds" for the blue wash glazing.

Step #5: The final step involves applying white to three facets: pure white to the facet at 11 o'clock, and a gray value to the two adjacent facets. To complete the rendering, apply watercolor varnish to accentuate the depth and richness of the sapphire. Plate 36 also indicates five steps leading to a fully rendered sapphire cabochon. This process parallels the previous one with some variations: in Step 1, the blue wash is applied; Step #2 introduces a lower value, in this case a darker blue to the upper left area in a half-moon shape; in Step #3, the reflected light is added, a high white value in the shape of an inverted comma at the bottom right of the stone; Step #4 consists of glazing the entire surface with a blue wash; Step #5, the incidental light consists of two round dots of pure white at the top, the upper dot combined with a gray "tail" fading toward the bottom; and again, an application of watercolor varnish. The various sapphire shapes are further illustrated with eleven examples, including: a faceted cushion shape, a tapered baguette, a star cabochon, and a buffed-top cushion shape.

Plates #37 and 38 are dedicated to the emerald and ruby, and follow Plate #36 with identical detailing.

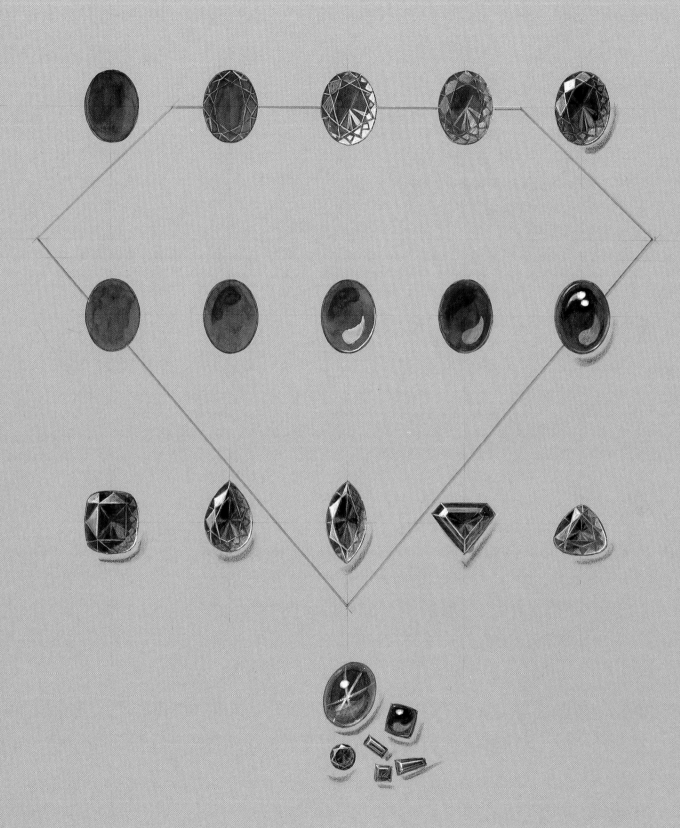

PLATE 37. PRECIOUS COLORED GEMSTONES: Ruby

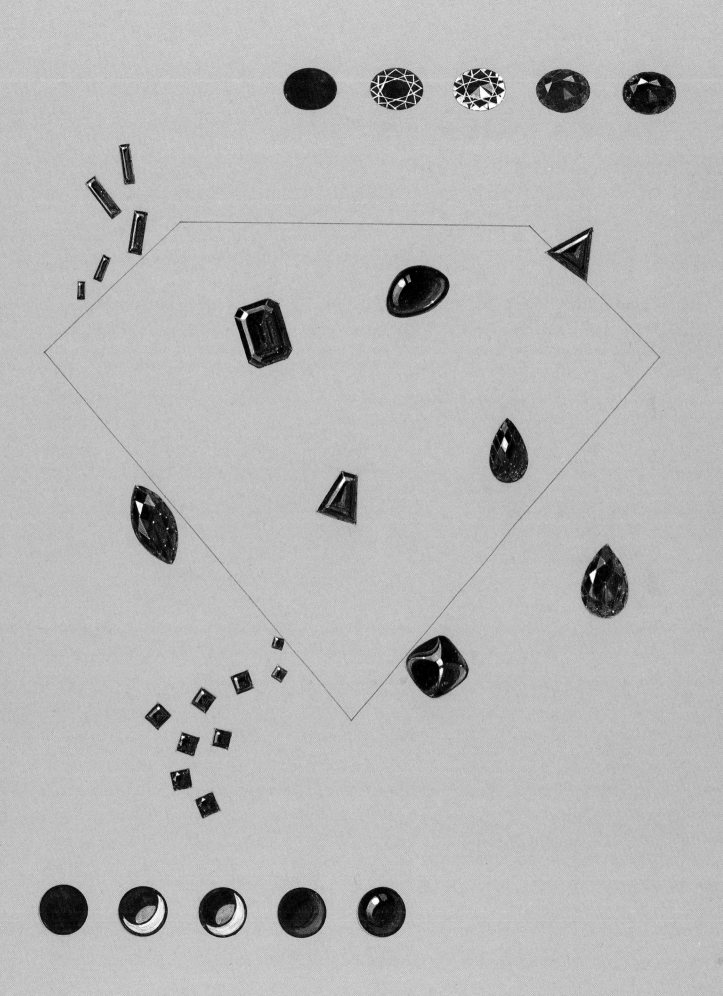

PLATE 38. PRECIOUS COLORED GEMSTONES: Emerald

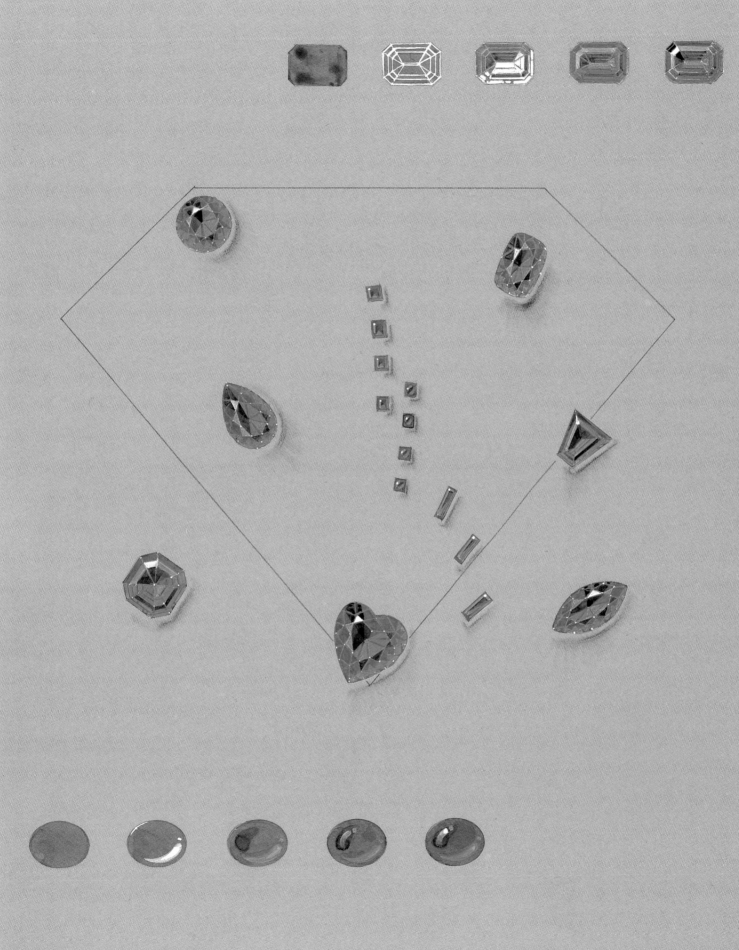

PLATE 39. COLORED GEMSTONES: Faceted and Cabochon

Gemstones are by no means less valuable than precious gemstones from an artistic point of view. In fact, their considerable color variety offers a great deal of possibilities to the creative mind. Faceted or cabochon, they can be of a clear or opaque nature, the opaque stones practically always in a cabochon form. Gemstones are also found in greater quantity and therefore are more readily available. Plate 39 illustrates a palette of transparent gemstones, twelve types most often used in jewelry. The rendering technique is based on the same glazing process previously demonstrated, with the appropriate base color applied as a first wash, and again, as a final or glazing step.

To illustrate the total number of gemstones in existence would be a senseless, although entertaining endeavor. Students should refer to books available on gemstones, a few of which are listed in the reference section. Observing the illustration, clockwise from the bottom left, the smaller palette illustrates: amethyst, rubellite, blue tourmaline, tsavorite, tanzanite, and aquamarine. On the larger palette, from the bottom: peridot, garnet, pink tourmaline, spinel, topaz and citrine. The color nuances of these stones can vary from lighter to darker hues. However, to establish a workable parameter, we have chosen the most common color of each gem.

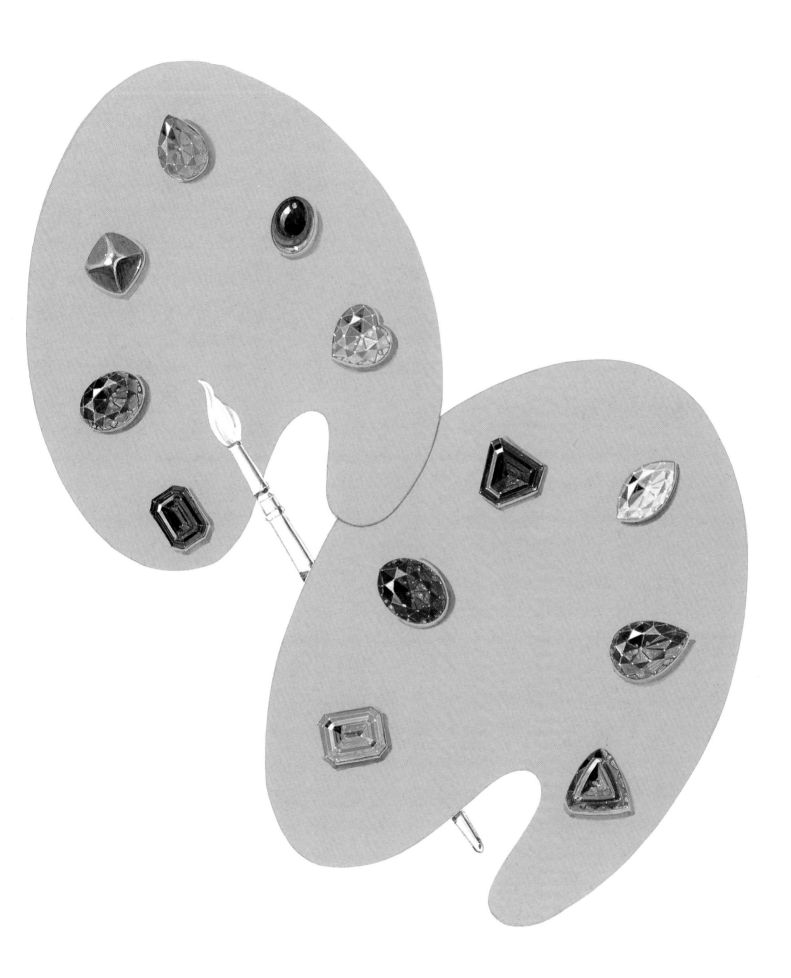

PLATE 40. OPAQUE GEMSTONES: Cabochons

Plate 40 illustrates a palette with fourteen opaque to transparent cabochons. They are, from the bottom left: black onyx (opaque), angel skin coral (opaque), chrysoprase (opaque), cat's eye (translucent), tiger's eye (translucent), lapis lazuli (opaque), turquoise (opaque), malachite (opaque), black opal (opaque), star rose quartz (translucent), and fire opal (translucent).

Recently, jewelry manufacturers are making extensive use of colored gemstones. Many of these "buffed tops" stones are adapted in various shapes to rings, necklaces, brooches, earrings and bracelets.

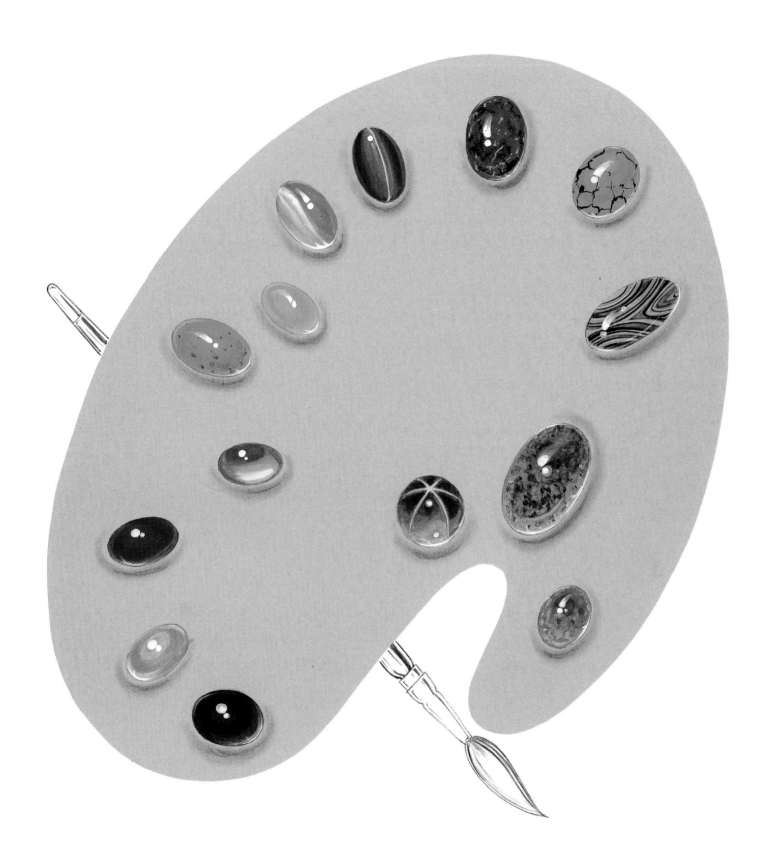

PLATE 41. PEARLS: Baroque, South Sea and Fresh Water

Pearls, sometimes referred to as "Jewels of the Sea," are available in many colors, from white to pink, to cream to black, and also vary in shape from round to Baroque. In spite of these differences, one particularity is common to all of them: the soft, almost iridescent quality of their "skin," known as the "orient" of the pearl. The rendering of the pearl requires a delicate handling of the different values and tones. The glow of the pearl must be obtained through the use of "wet tones" blending into one another, avoiding any hard definition. This technique is demonstrated in four steps on Plate 41.

Step #1: involves the tracing of the pearl and adding a circular low value with a graphite-darkened stump in the upper left area.

Step #2: Apply a diluted white wash over the whole surface of the pearl.

Step #3: Add a lighter value in circular form for the incidental light at the upper left, and a crescent shape for the reflected light at the right.

Step #4: Step 4 involves the final touch of a pure white dot within the circular high value at the left, and reinforcing the reflected light at the right.

Plate 41 illustrates an assortment of pearls: black, gold and dark gray round pearls, a Baroque and three fresh water pearls; also a graduated flow of round pearls and a tear-shaped pearl. This plate displays the very subtle nature of color variations in the pearl. The initial wash determines the color of the pearl, with the reflected light strengthening that color in the final step. The highlights, in the form of white dots, will remain identical. Concentrating on the "soft" approach of the rendering should be the primary concern from a technical point of view. Last but not least, a pearl should never be outlined by a thick line, as this would cancel the intended volume and give the pearl a pasty look instead of the desired iridescence.

PLATE 42 and 43. PERSPECTIVE: Faceted Round Stone at Various Angles

The three-dimensional aspect of a drawing affects all the components of that design, which includes the rendering of the stones. Perspective will dictate the appropriate shapes of the stones as they appear at various angles.

Plate 42 illustrates a faceted round stone in six different positions. The top left stone offers a minimized distortion as far as perspective is concerned. It is a side view displaying details of the crown and pavilion of the stone.

The bottom left stone, a top view, is a perfect circle with minimal perspective alterations in the crown facets.

The high, medium and low values delineate the specific volume of each stone in their respective positions. The best way to understand stones in perspective is to sketch them in as many angles as possible, drawing the crown facets as we have done in this illustration.

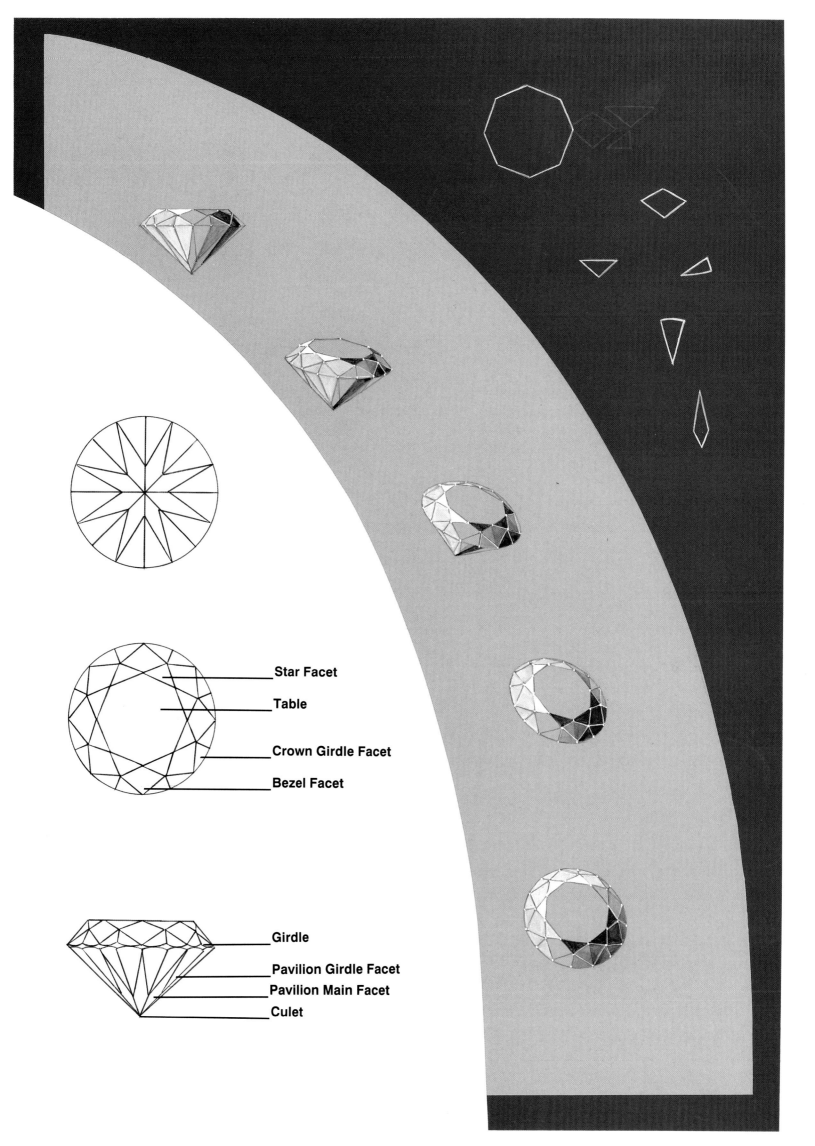

Star Facet

Table

Crown Girdle Facet

Bezel Facet

Girdle

Pavilion Girdle Facet

Pavilion Main Facet

Culet

PLATE 43. PERSPECTIVE: PAVE STONE PLACEMENT

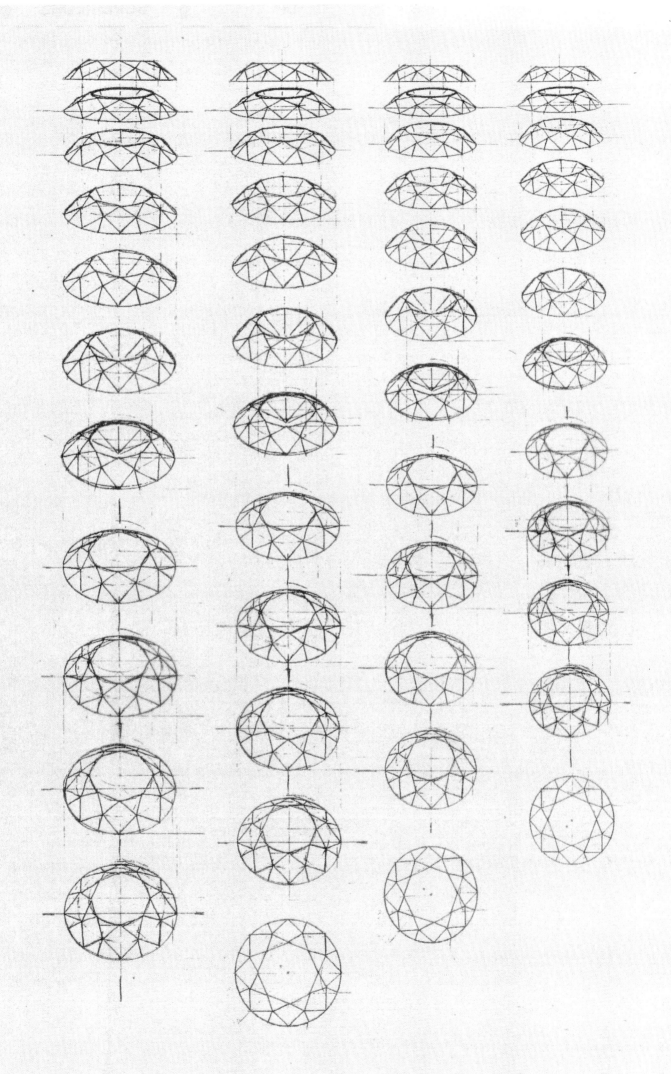

PLATE 44. PAVÉ STONE PLACEMENT II

Coined from the old French cobblestone paving of streets, pavé surfaces have been a staple of our trade for well over a century. As its etymology suggests, the stones on a pavé element are very closely set, covering the surface with a substantial amount of stones. Generally, these stones range in size from a minimum of three points to a maximum of fifteen points.

A crucial aspect of pavé rendering is the correct positioning of stones according to the surface and volume of the element. To illustrate this, a line drawing technique is used in Plate 44, with a few added values in pencil, to suggest the intended volume.

In Figure 1, to simplify the handling of pavé in perspective, our diagram deals with a single row of stones in a simulated band ring. The parallel lines originate from the curved line, at equal distances. When these lines are transferred to the top view, their spacing is altered by the curved surface.

This alteration in turn is reflected in the shape of the stone (circle) which becomes elliptical as it follows the curve. The more accentuated the curve, the narrower the ellipse.

Figure 2 reveals a line definition for positioning stones to achieve an optimal pavé surface. Whenever possible, this method should be applied, since it reduces the amount of metal left between the stones, allowing for a tight setting that best highlights the stones.

In Figure 3, the leaf shape illustrates the two steps involved in laying out a correct pavé element. The right side of the leaf consists of a line definition of the stone's positioning. These structural lines follow the volume of the surface. The left side of the leaf shows stones traced according to the perspective reflected in the structural lines.

Another important aspect of pavé indicated is the tapering of the stone sizes which are dictated by the shape and volume of the element, in this case the curves and tapering of the leaf.

The next illustration, Figure 4, shows a less desirable pavé method, albeit possible for a pavé treatment. Here, the shape of a half-tubular tapered element is paved where the stones are lined up in a straight fashion, row after row. Thus, the considerable amount of metal left between each stone is detrimental to the pavé, resulting in a duller look.

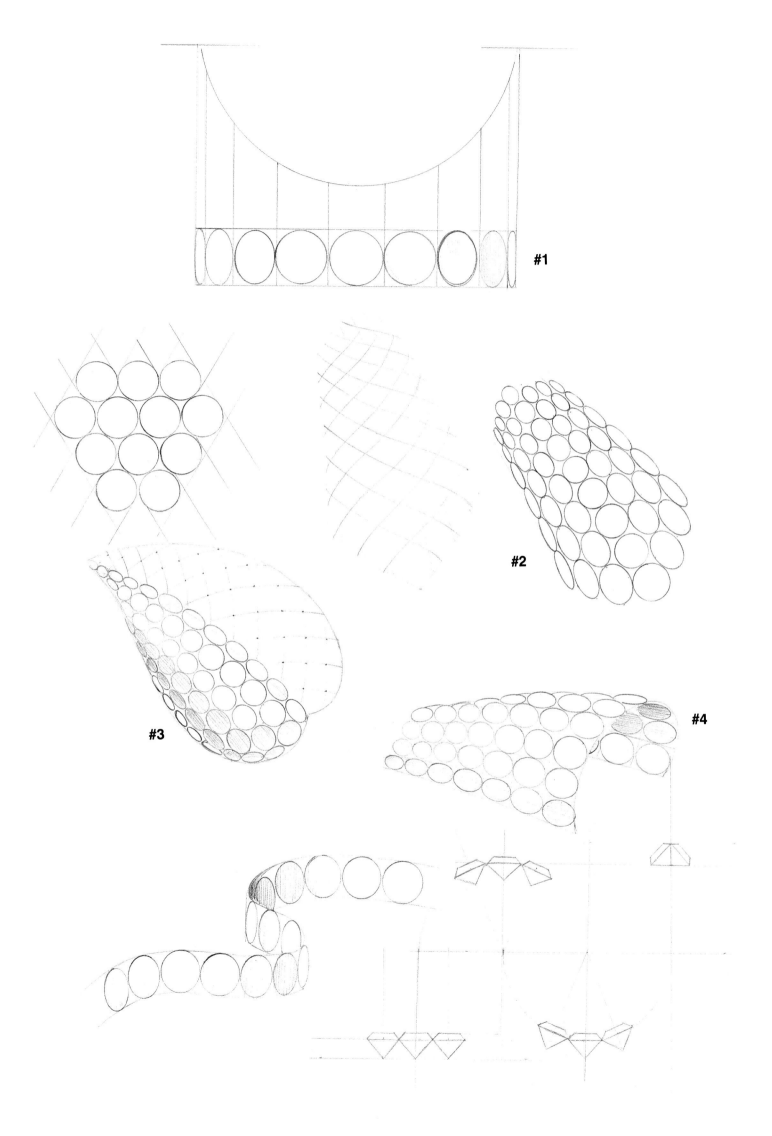

#1

#2

#3

#4

PLATE 45. PAVÉ: Step by Step Rendering Technique

Plate 45 illustrates the step-by-step rendering of a pavé leaf. First, the basic shape is outlined in pencil. Next, the low values are applied. These are followed by the light values, and finally, the stones are traced in white gouache according to the volume. White dots are then added between the stones to simulate the setting beads.

At the bottom of the plate, four pavé leaves indicate various volume possibilities, including domed, flat undulating, concave and convex surfaces.

PLATE 46. BAGUETTES AND CALIBRÉS

Once more, we consult the French dictionary to find the original meaning of this particular word. A baguette could define quite a few objects: from a wooden strip to a form of long, thin French bread, from a conductor's baton to a rectangular and narrow stone. Here, for obvious reasons, we are concerned with the last interpretation.

Plate 46 exemplifies the various ways in which baguettes are used. All these examples underline the very fluid nature of this cut. For the most part, they are set in groups, lending themselves to ribbon-like shapes, cascading or undulating elements such as the ballerina setting located at the bottom left of the plate. They can also be grouped individually, as in the earring with tapered baguettes. Below, straight baguettes set in flexible strips evoke a cascading effect.

A variant of the baguette, the calibré, meaning "cut to a specific size" in French, is illustrated in the channel set strips at the bottom of the plate. The top strip consists of regular calibrés with straight facets, while the lower is an example of the "princess" calibré, of recent origin, with "brilliant" faceting increasing the radiancy of the diamond.

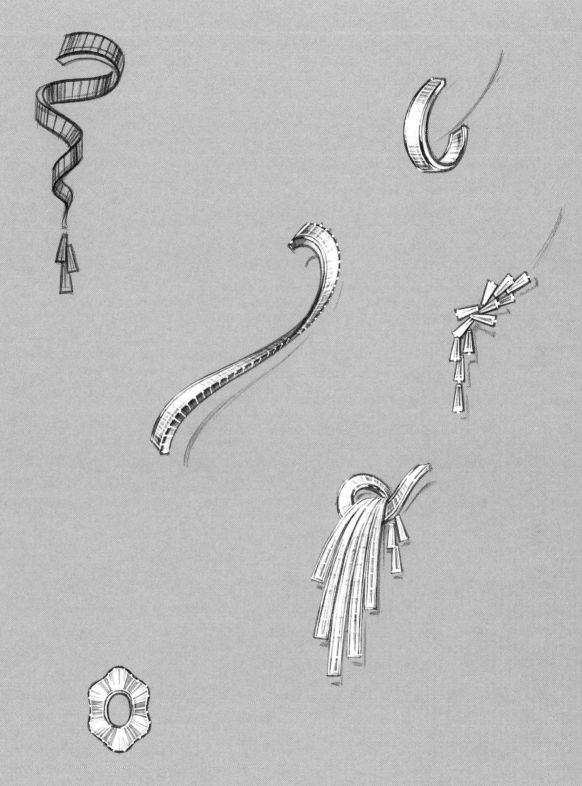

PLATE 47. VARIOUS SETTINGS FOR THE ROUND STONE

Among the great variety of gem shapes, the round stone remains the most affected by its setting. Plate 47 illustrates twelve variations of an identical element set with round diamonds. In these examples, the diamonds are set in platinum, which is the metal most commonly used in diamond pieces, though the same settings could be made in yellow gold for gems such as rubies, emeralds and other warm-colored stones.

Starting with the top row, from left to right, the first element is a classic bead set finished with a bright-edge cut. The second example shows a channel setting, the stones held solely by the walls on each side. The third element is a bezel setting, where each stone retains its shape due to the absence of prongs.

The second row features three scalloped elements. The first combines beads and half bezels. The beads set the stones on the inside line while the half-bezels hold the stone on the outside. The second element shows the stones set in a scalloped plate to which prongs have been soldered, a large prong holding two stones on the inside, and a smaller holding each stone centered on the outside. The third element varies by an additional prong between each stone on the outside.

The third row starts with a straight bar or Gemlock setting, with the stones secured on either side by a metal strip. The second element is a classic four- prong setting, the third example is a three-prong setting.

The bottom row shows examples of fancy settings. The stones in the first element are set by a slanted bar. The second element shows a weaved setting where each stone is set by a curving prong. The last element combines both channels and prongs with the two outer prongs set close to each other.

To conclude, the various settings illustrated demonstrate how specific settings can be instrumental in creating distinct looks in a jewel; from a tailored channel or bead set element to the more flowery silhouette of a scalloped piece, or from a compact tube setting to the flowing lines of a weaved element.

PLATE 48. GROUPING FANCY SHAPE STONES

The examples in Plate 48 deal with a particular type of jewel made entirely of individual stones, mostly marquise or pear- shapes, prong-set in platinum or gold. This type of jewelry is associated with such famous houses as Harry Winston, Van Cleef & Arpels and Tiffany, to name but a few. It is also what has been classified by Europeans as "haute joaillerie," reflecting the high quality of both labor and stones.

Unlike metal, which offers a great deal of possibilities in the ways it can be shaped or designed, stones remain singular entities which must be assembled and worked into creative forms and volumes.

The grouping of fancy shape stones, as it pertains to the elegance of line and movement, is best defined by the need to angle each stone in connection with the direction or flow of the design.

The six designs illustrated in Plate 48 demonstrate this principle, with arrows indicating the various angles of the stones. The three pendant earring designs, Figures 1, 2 & 3, which are built around a pear-shape stone, exemplify how the surrounding smaller stones are studies in multiple angles. No stone parallels another in its angle (with the exception of the vertical axis), allowing for the flow of the design and avoiding any rigidity or crowding of the pattern. Figure 4 shows a type of bursting pattern designed around a center point from which all the angles evolve in their specific directions. Figures 5 & 6 are derived from a leaf pattern. In these two classic designs, one can see the importance of stone placement, and how any deviation from this would affect the composition.

We recommend the use of lines as a guide for checking the angles of stones in the preliminary stages of designing this type of jewelry. The use of negative space definition (refer to Plate 7) would be an added checking process for successful designing.

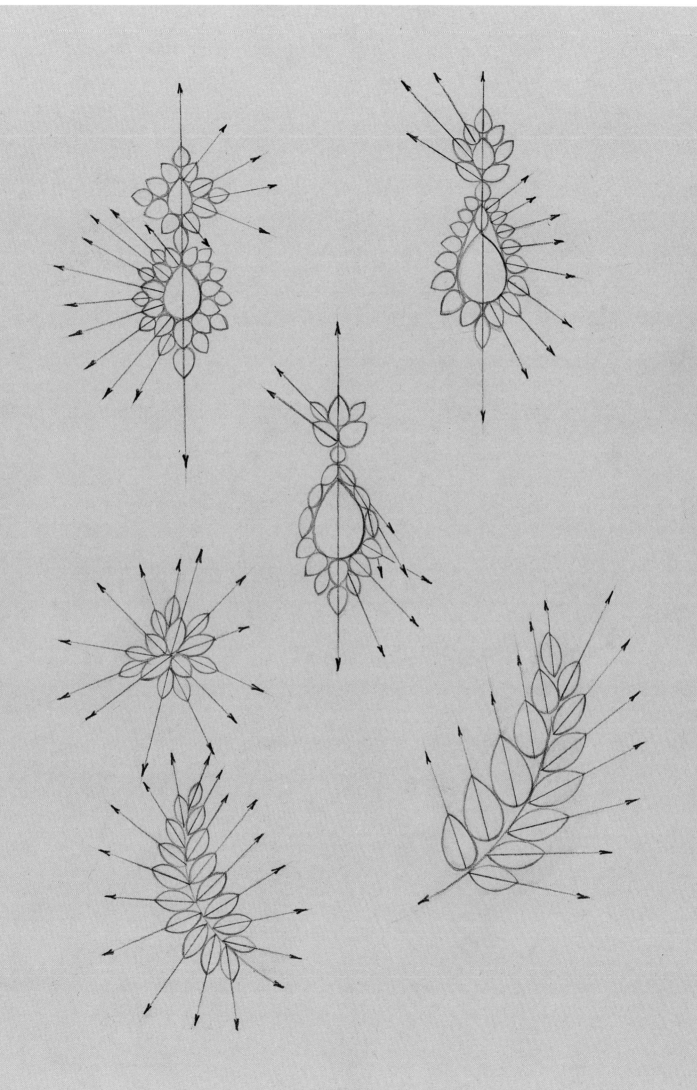

PLATE 49. INTRODUCTION TO THE RING

The ring is, without a doubt, the most popular form of jewelry. Indeed, it has an intriguing past laced with mystery and magic spanning centuries.

This adornment, although modest in size, has generated symbolic implications unmatched in the world of jewels: power, wealth, fidelity, luck and immortality. From its inception, it has been a constant companion to both men and women, and a means of self-gratification as well as a personal status symbol.

The first rings were carved out of bone and ornamented with superficial engraving, probably related to some esoteric meaning.

Around 3,000 BC, in the area of Mesopotamia, we find the oldest examples of metal rings, in bronze, a new alloy representing a major achievement in the development of metalsmithing.

Gold appeared in Egypt around 2500 BC, and acquired from the very start a prevalent status in jewelry, a status that silver and iron, discovered subsequently, were not able to alter. Malleability, resistance to oxidation and color are the properties that made gold the "regal" metal and perfect vehicle for the craftsman.

Plate 48 illustrates a bold modern diamond ring juxtaposed against a background of metal rings derivative of early ring styles.

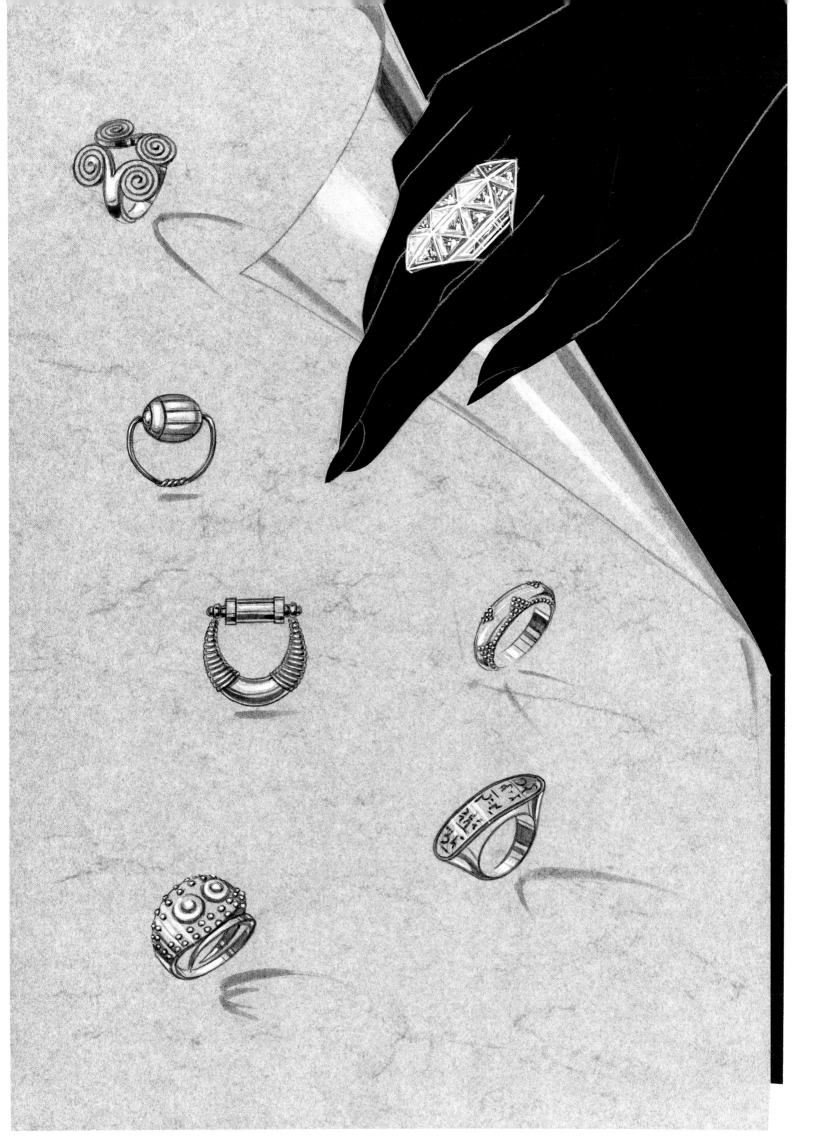

PLATE 50. MECHANICAL DRAWING

Plate 50 illustrates the mechanical drawing or "shop" rendering of three basic ring shapes: a rectangular "signet" ring, a domed ring, and a narrow band ring. This type of drawing is done primarily to supply the jeweler with a precise graphic description of the ring's details as they appear on the top and sides of the jewel.

Since the method used in these three examples is identical, the "signet" ring alone will be examined in this step-by-step demonstration.

Step #1: consists in the tracing of the top-view, which determines both the length and width of the "ring's head," in this case the rectangle, and the overall length of the ring according to the finger size. The tracing of the tapering shank on both sides of the "head" complete the top view.

Step #2: Vertical parallel lines are extended downward from the center of the "head," the rectangle length and the whole length of the top-view.

Step #3: The circle corresponding to the finger size is traced on the vertical centerline.

Step #4: The height or thickness of the "head" is established by a horizontal line extending to the length of the rectangle.

Step #5: The shank is traced on both sides of the "head," tapering toward the bottom of the circle. The first side-view is completed.

The second side-view is established as follows:

Step #1: Three horizontal parallel lines are extended toward the right of the top-view from the center and width of the "head." Step 2. An intersecting line at a 45-degree angle is traced across the three horizontal lines.

Step #3: Three vertical parallel lines are projected downward from the points intersecting at the 45-degree line.

Step #4: Two horizontal parallel lines are extended to the right from the top and bottom of side-view #1.

Step #5: The two dotted lines are used to indicate the diameter of the finger size.

Step #6: The tapering part of the shank is traced, starting at the top. From these points the shank tapers to the bottom horizontal line. The second side-view is now completed.

To maintain a maximum accuracy in the transferring process of these various measures, *keep the three views relatively close to each other* to avoid errors due to an over-extension of the vertical and horizontal lines.

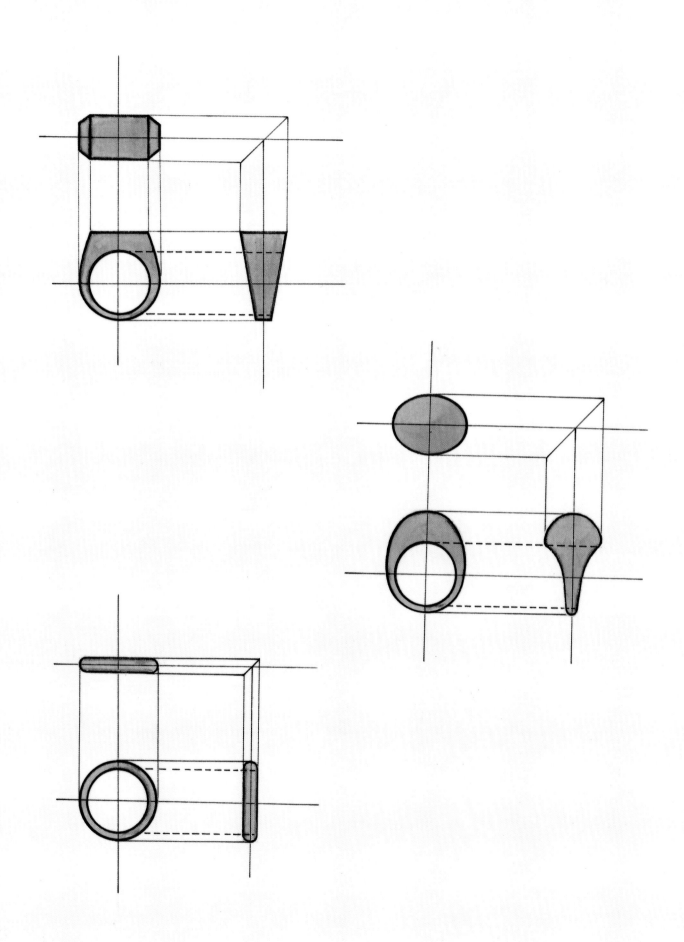

PLATE 51. THREE-QUARTER VIEW (Pencil Line Drawing)

A three-quarter view has the distinct advantage of exposing three views of a ring in one design, thus offering a more realistic portrayal of the jewel. This form of presentation is evidently the least time-consuming, and therefore the most practiced.

Illustrated in eight consecutive steps, the structural lines in the first seven steps have been left to preserve the continuity in the "building up" of the ring. We trust the clarity demonstrated in the steps to be the best possible guide to understanding the three-quarter perspective, and will now delineate the various steps:

Rectangular Top Ring

Step #1: Front ellipse traced at 45-degree angle; length of ellipse: 16.5 mm, equivalent to a 6 finger size.

Step #2: Two parallel lines set parameter for the back ellipse.

Step #3: Back ellipse opens in relation to the tapering of the shank and the width of the rectangle.

Step #4: Tracing of center axis of ring's top.

Step #5: Determine thickness of ring's top at the center axis.

Step #6: Tracing of rectangular top.

Step #7: Completion of shank and ring sides.

Step #8: Finished drawing, with structural lines removed.

Domed Ring

The steps here are similar, with the exception of steps #5, #6, and #7 where the width of the ring's top exceeds the dimension of the two el-lipses.

Step #5: Determine height of dome at center axis.

Step #6: Front ellipse modified to accommodate the width of the dome.

Step #7: Dome and shank completed relative to height and width.

Step #8: Finished drawing, with structural lines removed.

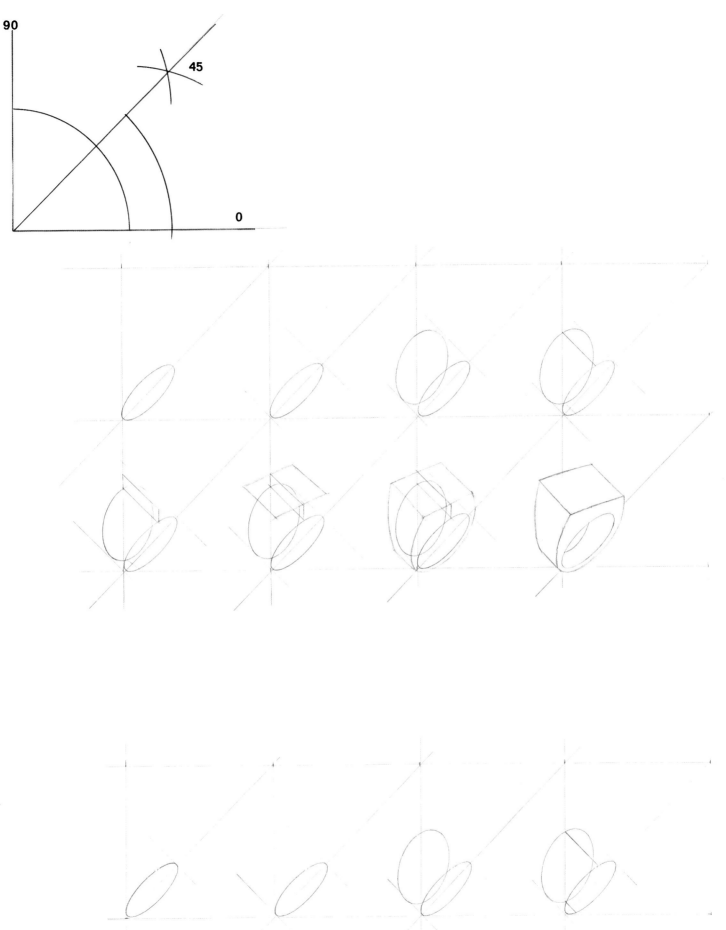

PLATE 52. SOLITAIRE. Pencil Mechanical (Ink & Full Rendering)

One of the best known rings, the solitaire or "engagement" ring, offers a rather modest field for creative interpretation. As a rule, the design is traditionally defined by the use of a single stone, a diamond, which limits the designer to the adornment of a single setting mounted on a shank. Variations can be obtained through the number of prongs setting the stone and the ornamentation of bezels.

Plate 52 illustrates an enlarged three-quarter view of a classic Cartier six-prong setting ring, mounted on a straight rectangular shank. The other illustrations show an identical solitaire, where the top drawing indicates the rendering in four steps, and the other depicts a "mechanical" drawing. In this latter example, while the setting remains a six-prong classic, the shank is a "knife-edge" and tapers as it joins the setting. This is meant to enhance the stone by minimizing the amount of visible metal.

Solitaire shanks can be of various types, such as square, half-round, knife-edge, bezeled, gouged or split, scalloped, to cite a few of the most common styles. As a rule, they should be tapered toward the back ensuring the elegance of the ring. The sheer simplicity of solitaire mountings requires a thorough understanding of the ring's proportions.

From the designer's drawing to the jeweler's bench, the proportions between the prong's bezel and shank must merge into a final effect to best set off the diamond. At a time when solitaire rings were entirely hand-made, it was customary to test a newly hired jeweler with a six-prong mounting.

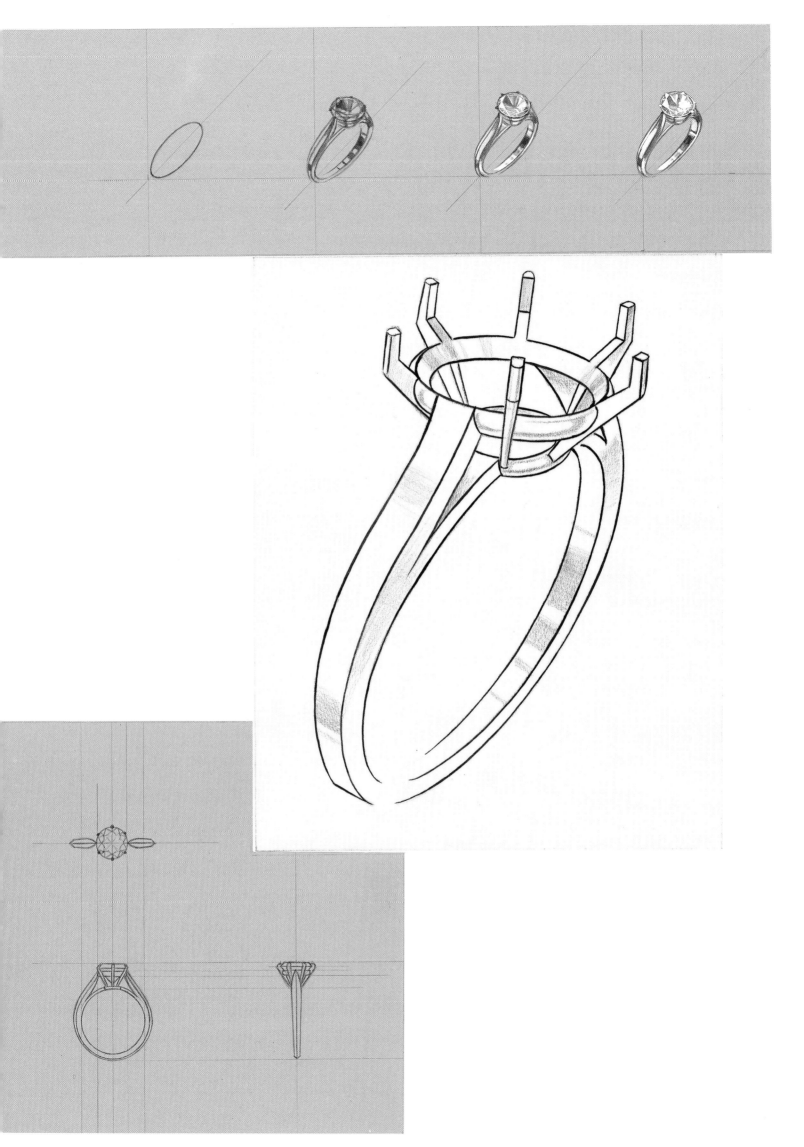

PLATE 53. SOLITAIRE: Fancy Settings

Plate 53 illustrates seven solitaire ring designs, rendered from side views to best expose the settings. At center, the classic "Tiffany" setting has six scalloped prongs, minimizing the visible metal to the advantage of the diamond. For aesthetic reasons, white metals are seldom worked into elaborate patterns when dealing with all-diamond jewelry, where the purpose is essentially to show stones.

For this very reason, the other designs in Plate 53 have been worked in yellow gold, a metal much better appropriated to elaborate settings. These rings make use of decorative prong settings and shank types, as in Plate 52. The various forms of ornamentation possible must be compact enough to remain structurally sound and maintain the strength of the prongs.

PLATE 54. DIAMOND SOLITAIRE WITH SIDE STONES

Plate 54 illustrates nine variations of a diamond solitaire ring. These rings are mounted in platinum and embellished with side stones. They synthesize the A-B-C's of the designer's approach to this type of ring and underline the important part played by the balance of the center stone vis-a-vis the side stones.

In every case, the center stone remains the primary focus and must not be overpowered by the side stones. However, observing this relationship should not bring the opposite result, where the side elements become too weak and give the ring a "puny" look. These additional stones, which are set either in prongs or in a flat shank, enhance, within feasible proportions, the look of these rings. The center stone is subject to variations, both in size and shape, and for all intents and purposes, the designs could also work around a marquise, pear-shape, or emerald-cut center stone.

PLATE 55. TWISTED SHANK RING

Although the most common shank is straight, there are alternative configurations such as the "S"-shaped shanks which present attractive departures from the traditional looks illustrated in Plate 54.

The "S"-shaped rings on the extended and folded hand demonstrate the adaptability of this ring type to the pinky finger. Evidently, the "S" must be shaped according to the hand the ring is worn on, twisting left or right accordingly.

The twisted shank lends itself well to asymmetrical designs as well as symmetrical compositions. Its versatility is further demonstrated in the following plate.

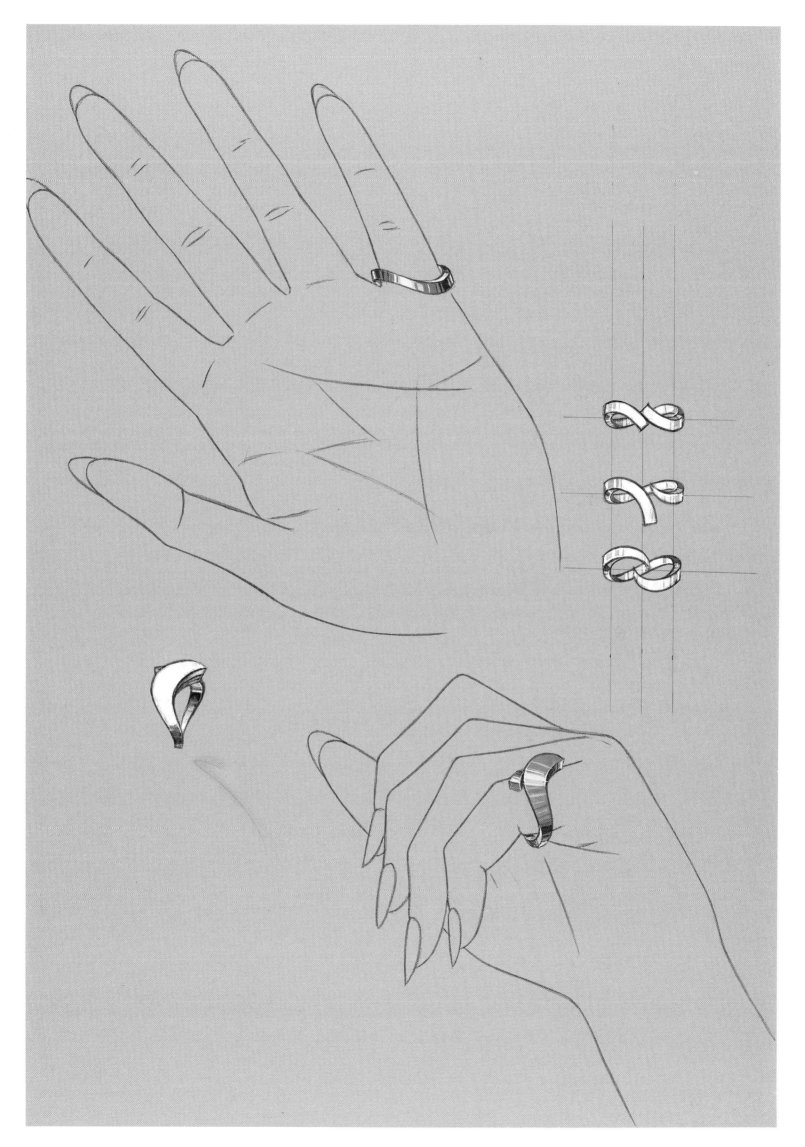

PLATE 56. TWISTED SHANK RING II (Pencil Sketches)

The seven pencil sketches in Plate 56 indicate how the basic dynamic of the twist can be interpreted into different designs. With one exception, all the rings are asymmetrical, and because of this, a top view of the ring will be helpful in determining the exact position of the stones.

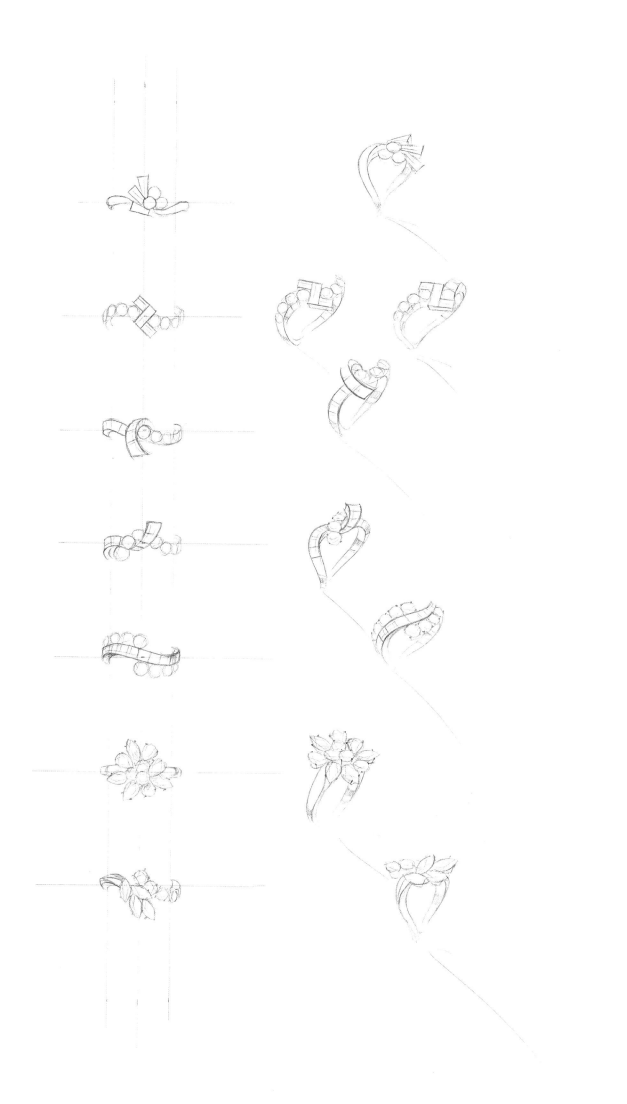

PLATE 57. PERSPECTIVE: Viewpoint of a Ring

Plate 57 emphasizes an important aspect of design and presentation, the choice of a viewpoint that best exposes the predominant features of the ring, i.e., top or side details.

In the illustration, a ring is shown both in a shop drawing, and on the radius from six perspectives.

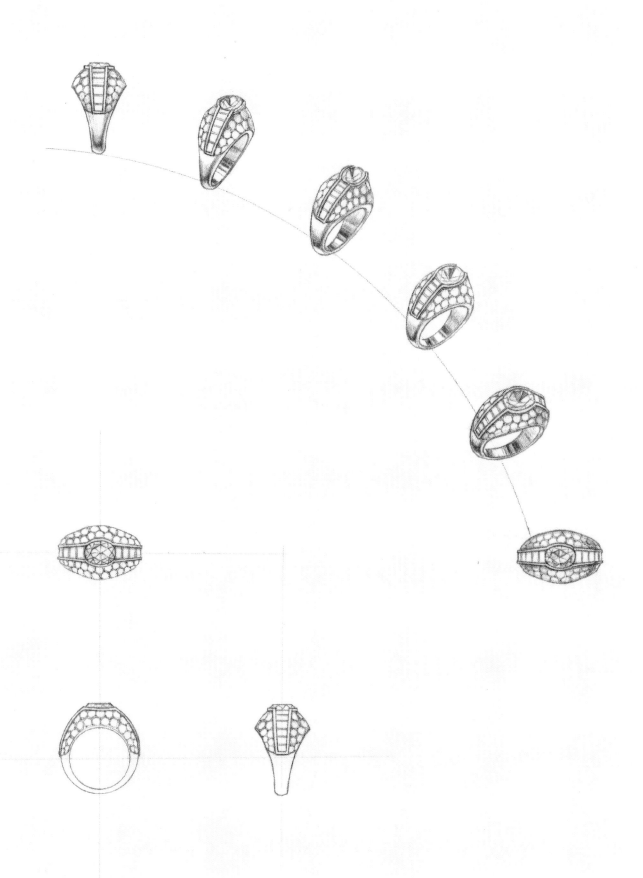

PLATE 58. THREE-QUARTER VIEW OF A RING (Step-by-Step Rendering)

In Plate 58, six steps are shown from the pencil tracing to the finished rendering. A close study of each step is the basis for assimilating this technique. Nonetheless, we will describe the step-by-step process in order to cover every aspect of the rendering.

Step #1: Pencil tracing.

Step #2: Application of medium value *Monaco Yellow* over gold element; light wash over pavé areas; red wash over ruby.

Step #3: Pavé areas reinforced with white, with the exception of row adjacent to finger opening. Deep red value applied to left side of ruby; reflected light *Cadmium Yellow Deep* applied to right and left sides of the shank. Medium-dark value *Light Brown* applied on either side of the fluted shank element inside the shank.

Step #4: A medium light value *Golden Yellow* & White is added to the fluting, the inside of the shank, and also on the part of the bezel exposed to the light.

Step #5: A red glaze is applied over the ruby. The pavé areas are reinforced with white wash. Pure white dots between the stones indicate the setting beads. The dark value *Van Dyke Brown* is applied to areas next to the reflected lights and the inside shank.

Step #6: The ruby is highlighted with white. The highest gold values *Cadmium Yellow* & White are applied to the fluting, bezel and inside shank. To complete the rendering, a gray shadow is added at the base of the ring for a three-dimensional effect.

PLATE 59. THE GOLD RING

Modern or contemporary gold rings are identifiable by a certain bulk in their proportions which allows for a more tailored look, fit for everyday wear. The challenge of designing "tailored" rings, with the absence of stones, requires that the designer finds other means for embellishment. In Plate 58, the five rings illustrated are consistent in style by the use of scalloped or fluted elements in their design. The area of interest in these rings is enhanced by the reflective quality of the fluted surfaces, which become a focusing point in their ornamentation.

PLATE 60. FANCY CENTER STONE DIAMOND & GOLD RINGS

Plate 60 features rings with fancy center stones of various shapes. These designs are a first step toward the "cocktail" ring seen in the following plates. The purpose here was to avoid the look of the engagement ring while preserving the identity of the center stone in the context of a more elaborate setting, which involves the use of pavé elements and fancy cut stones.

Though the overall design appears substantial, the complementary elements remain subordinate to the center stone. Notice that the pavé surfaces introduced in the rings, whether wrapped around or as lateral motifs, do not antagonize the center stone.

PLATE 61. VARIATIONS ON A BASIC SHAPE

Plate 61 demonstrates how a simple basic ring shape can be expanded into fourteen distinct designs. On a professional level, creating variations on a given theme is frequently encountered. In addition to the diversification of a model, it offers the manufacturer leeway in terms of stones, labor and cost.

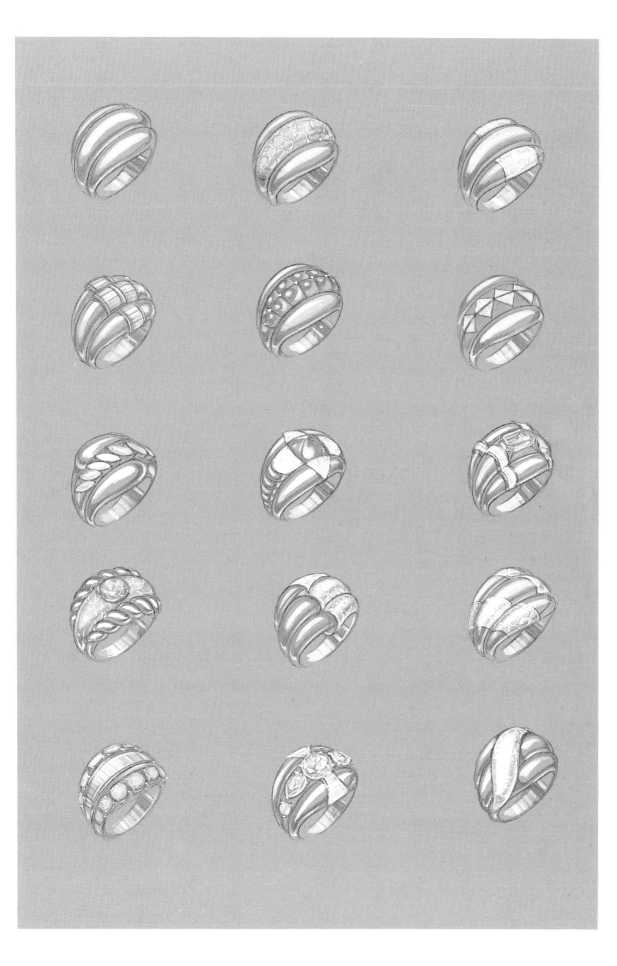

PLATE 62. LARGE CENTER STONE

When dealing with rings of the type illustrated in Plate 62, the large center stone, by its nature, needs a minimal addition of metal or other stones. The ornamentation should appear on each side of the setting at an angle studied to avoid the broadening of the ring, which both aesthetically and practically must not exceed certain parameters to be both wearable and elegant. Viewed from the top, these side elements nestle under the center stone, adding just the right contrast.

PLATE 63. "ENTOURAGE" RINGS

The word "entourage," borrowed from the French verb "entourer," literally means "to surround." Plate 63 illustrates eight entourage rings. As a rule, the precious colored gems in this type of ring are surrounded by a uniform and often symmetrical border of stones meant to intensify their color through contrast, with the exception of the all-diamond entourage, where the contrast is established through the use of smaller stones.

In designing entourage rings, one technical aspect to be considered is the height of the center stone pavilion. That dimension can vary in colored stones and sometimes be disproportionate to the crown. The pavilion must be covered by the entourage, where one, two and sometimes three rows of stones might be required for that purpose. Thus, the freedom in interpretation is conditioned by this factor, as the "entourage" should never be left floating around the center stone.

PLATE 64. ASYMMETRICAL FANCY RINGS

Asymmetry in stone cutting is a fairly common practice in colored gems where the color repartition is often irregular. To obtain optimal color intensity and maximum carat weight, the lapidary often decides on an asymmetrical cut. Many spectacular gems were cut in that fashion, albeit departing from the classic approach in their shape and faceting.

Stone asymmetry offers an exceptional opportunity for the designer to depart from the *deja vu,* giving full measure to his or her creativity. In general terms, designs can either follow the shape and size of stones or contrast them. Occasionally, a symmetrical stone can be mounted in an asymmetrical setting. The seven fancy ring designs in Plate 64 illustrate these various types of mountings.

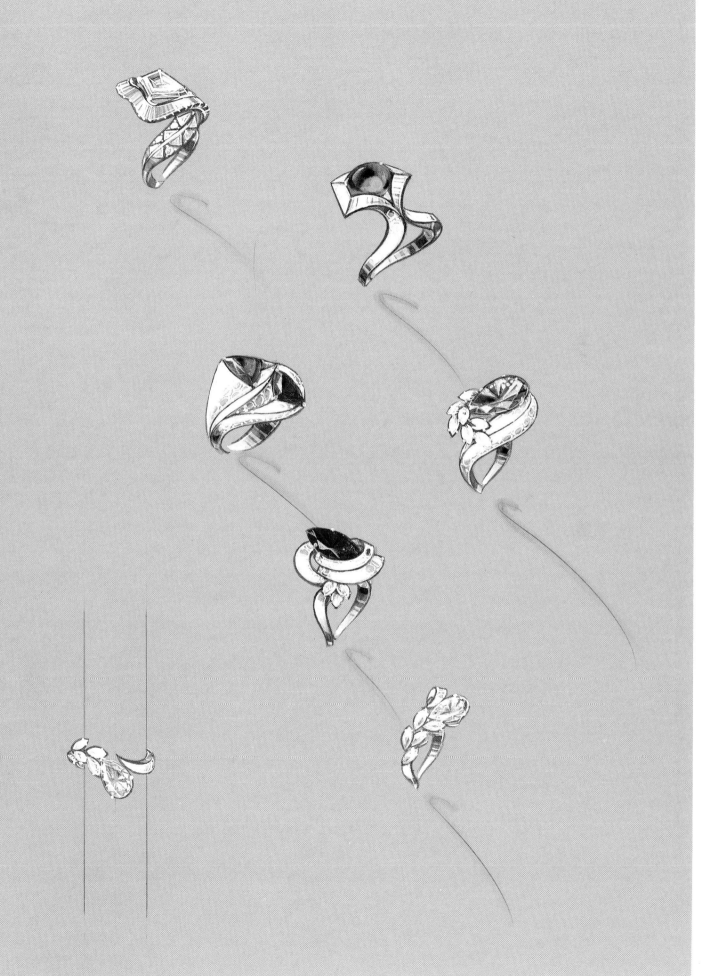

PLATE 65. CLASSIC COCKTAIL RING

The evolution of ring styles has been influenced by both fashion and evolving techniques. The increased availability of colored gemstones and diamonds has resulted in the extended use of stones and mixing of colors and bulkier rings. The cocktail ring apparently derives its name from such a trend. The primary value of this ring genre is founded on the originality of the designs.

The seven examples in Plate 65 are typical cocktail ring designs, the styles of which originated in the 1930's and 40's. It should be specified that large colored stones mounted in these kinds of rings are seldom of gem quality. If this were the case, these stones would have been set in "entourage" or "center stone" mountings.

PLATE 66. INVISIBLE-SET RINGS

The invisible-set technique is a relatively recent development resulting from a collaborative effort between jewelers and lapidaries to create the illusion of a field of colored gems devoid of metal. Van Cleef & Arpels was the first among the famous jewelry houses, at the Place Vendome in Paris, to raise this new look to its utmost elegance and popularity.

From a creative point of view, invisible-set jewels are characterized by the use of solid compact shapes of colored stones accentuated by diamond elements. The invisible-set element must be left whole in order to preserve its impact, and diamonds or any other stones are secondary to the invisible-set area. Typical forms for invisible setting techniques are smooth oval or roundish shapes and leaf-like patterns.

Plate 66 shows six rings which accurately reflect these principles. With the advent of the laser cutting technique, the princess cut diamond has been added to the classic ruby and sapphire jewels set in this mode. This new addition is illustrated by a very rich looking invisible-set princess cut diamond domed ring set in platinum.

PLATE 67. COLORED GEMSTONE RINGS

This type of ring predominantly consists of a large gemstone set in gold with occasional diamond detailing. Since the initial cost of these colored gemstones is quite lower, when compared to precious gems, this factor must be taken into consideration when creating their settings. The addition of large diamonds would definitely upset the mercantile advantages of these rings, which are primarily to offer style and color at an affordable price.

The six rings in Plate 67 display a variety of models using gemstones in stylized gold mountings, including two with diamond details.

PLATE 68. LARGE PEARL RINGS

Pearls come in a great variety of shapes, sizes and colors, which affects their cost. The designer must take this into account when devising a suitable mounting for the pearl or pearls.

Plate 68 illustrates eight pearls from twelve to sixteen millimeters set in ring mountings. In this type of ring, the pearl itself is the major statement, and the diamond accents are conditioned by the pearl size and quality.

The models reflect a variety of mountings relevant to the use of important pearls that range from a simple entourage of marquise diamonds to a more elaborate setting composed of a "skirt" of diamond baguettes contrasting with a "collerette" of round stones encircling the pearl, to one where color is introduced as a contrast by the use of two pear-shape rubies.

PLATE 69. MABE PEARL AND MOTHER OF PEARL RINGS

Although held in lesser regard by true pearl afficionados, mabe pearls are used extensively in jewelry by virtue of their affordability. Once more, cost considerations influence the designer in choice of materials and creative concepts: pavé surfaces are used over more expensive fancy shape stones; gold is chosen for the mounting of materials such as onyx, mother of pearl and coral, selected for their adaptability, cost and color- contrasting qualities.

The six rings in Plate 68 exemplify how "lesser" materials can be utilized to create inventive designs, carved into interesting shapes, and, in two instances, complement the mabe pearl. Some mabe pearls of unusual quality justify a lift in treatment obtained through the use of diamond motifs.

PLATE 70. SPECIAL-CUT STONE RING

In the past two decades, the progress achieved in the art of stone cutting has brought about a very diversified inventory of special-cut colored gemstones. This diversity has, in turn, allowed designers to exploit new avenues of creativity. Bulgari, among the best known houses, has made extensive use of special-cut gems adapted to their creations of flowing yet compact designs.

Special-cut gems are often embedded in the entire surface, particularly in ring designs, and, in this sense, are somewhat related to invisible-set jewels. In the illustration of six special-cut rings, Plate 70, five designs are in this style and one with the addition of diamonds.

Typical of special-cut gems, in most cases, their cut, is a semi-cabochon known as a "buff top" or "French puff." Also, the absence of facets adds to the pleasing softness of the volume well-fitted to contemporary designs.

PLATE 71. SPECIAL ORDER RING

Among the many areas familiar to the professional designer, special order work holds a significant place not to be underestimated. In the course of various inheritances and estate purchases, a great number of jewels must be remounted or altered for contemporary settings. Here, the creative challenge is restricted by the precision involved in transforming the existing material in a jewel, at times without any addition of stones.

Accordingly, Plate 71 illustrates an exact amount of diamonds to be mounted in a platinum ring setting. The three models shown are related through the presence of a large center pear-shape diamond, and an identical amount of stones, yet exhibit three distinctive looks.

Most jewelry firms are receptive to special order as long as the quality of the materials justifies the expense of a new mounting. The satisfaction of seeing a dated jewel reborn in an elegant contemporary one has frequently resulted in regular customers for these firms.

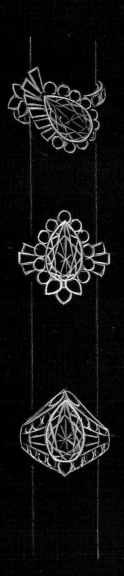

PLATE 72. MEN'S RINGS

Men's jewelry is mostly confined to four basic ornaments: the watch, the signet ring, the cuff-links and studs, and the tie bar. Name bracelets, gold chains and pendants represent but a minor percentage of the market for men's jewelry. To these we can add the wedding band, and for Americans, the ever popular college ring.

Specialty companies have flooded the market with catalogs on men's rings covering the gamut of classic variations. Notwithstanding, the challenge remains to create the "ultimate" new look in a man's ring. Recently, the introduction of special- cut stones have facilitated the task of designers to come up with fresh ideas.

The nine rings illustrated in Plate 71 explore this new direction in men's rings. The character of the rings remains simple and strong, since overworking the decorative motif would alienate most clients that have shown a preference toward more basic tailored designs.

PLATE 73. INTRODUCTION TO THE EARRING

Most consistent throughout centuries of human behavior, the need to adorn oneself has been pursued by both men and women. Among the various forms of adornment, jewelry has had an important role, and most interestingly, some styles dating back 4000 years are still popular today.

Although earrings have primarily been worn by women as jewelry, historically, they gained favor among men as symbols of power and honor during the Roman era. In the 17th century, a "Créole," or single hoop earring, was worn on the left ear by sailors crossing the perilous Cape Horn, in recognition of their accomplishments. This tradition, originating in the 17th century, recurred in the 18th and 19th centuries among craft guild members, such as the masons, as a form of recognition for their status of "Master" or "Companion."

PLATE 74. THE EARRING'S DYNAMIC PRINCIPLES

Earring designs follow various patterns, all directly influenced by the area they are meant to ornate. It is very important to consider the ear in relation to the face when creating an earring; the dynamic, volume, length and size of the elements composing the design must remain in proportion with the lobe and the general contour of the face, if the design is to be successful.

We are demonstrating with Plate 74 nine basic approaches to what we call an earring's dynamic, a guideline upon which concepts can be developed. The white arrows indicate the direction of the main movement or dynamic of the earring, while the black arrows offer a contrasting movement. The solid areas are meant to highlight the surface available to creative interpretations.

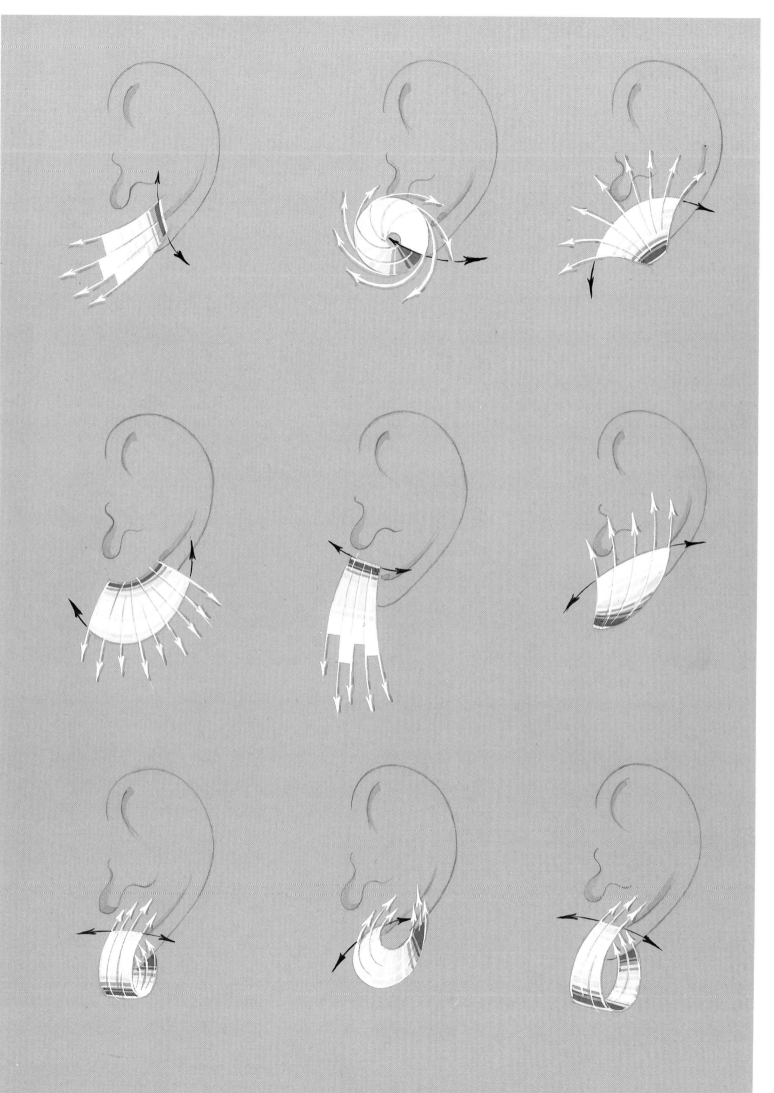

PLATE 75. DYNAMIC PRINCIPLES. GOLD EXAMPLES

The application of this dynamic principle is illustrated in Plate 75. Through the use of simple fluted elements we have kept our application as obvious as possible. Once the basic dynamic of the earring is set, the variations in the use of stones and metal become practically endless. Here, we are stressing the need to determine, from the very beginning, the "look" of the earring, thus establishing the basic structure and movement indispensable to further creative endeavors.

The visual weight of the various combined elements should also be well-balanced so as to support the dynamic of the initial concept, avoiding top or bottom heaviness. Starting with the simplest and clearest approach will always be most helpful in assimilating the various principles of sound designing, allowing for the further expansion of ideas.

PLATE 76. GOLD BUTTON EARRINGS

The great wearability of button earrings partially accounts for their popularity. Their compact nature, often highly domed, allows for both a frontal and side view on the face, a detail much appreciated by the wearer.

The term "button" should not confine the designer's creativity to a circular shape, determined by the fact that it is worn primarily on the lobe. The choice can be quite diversified to include cushion, octagonal, hexagonal, pentagonal, oval or amorphic forms. Strong angular shapes should be handled with care so as not to appear overly aggressive. Compact, simple elements carry the feeling of volume, as illustrated in the two designs on the right. The other three earrings, although more detailed, maintain a sufficient amount of visual strength, through binding the different textures.

PLATE 77. GOLD & DIAMOND BUTTON EARRINGS

The examples in Plate 77 depart from the very tailored gold earring and introduce a "richer" look through the use of diamonds and baguettes. The gold still represents about 50% of the total earring volume, a proportion that gives both the diamonds and gold elements a well-balanced visual weight. The maximum impact is achieved by grouping the diamonds in pavé ornaments, while using the baguettes in "framing" or "tied-over" ornaments. The overall look of these earrings is still quite compact, yet the important factor resides in the proper "dosage" of stones versus metal.

PLATE 78. GOLD & DIAMOND BUTTON EARRINGS

In Plate 78, with the further addition of fancies, pear-shape and marquise diamonds, the earrings depart from the gold look to a more platinum-type jewelry look. While the diamonds could stand on their own, the fine gold wires framing the stones soften the formal platinum look, giving the earring an extended option. Also, the use of gold wire which closely follows the stones' shape in most examples, used in this fashion, preserve and accentuate the identity of the fancies, sharply defining the contour of the earring. It is easy to overcrowd a design when working with fancies, the result being the loss of definition between the various shapes. To avoid such pitfalls, remember to make use of contrasting shapes, sizes and dynamics, and ultimately, check the positive-negative space.

PLATE 79. GOLD & DIAMOND EARRINGS

       With the same purpose of deformalizing an otherwise all- diamond earring, Plate 79 displays examples that make use of gold wire to form elements, creating independent patterns within the earring designs. These patterns, in turn, support the dynamic of the diamond elements. Here again, the identity of the fancies will play an important part in the overall composition when accentuated, as in designs #1, #3 and #5, or more closely regrouped, as in designs #2 and #4. In these designs, the statement definitely leans toward the stones, the last step before the all-diamond earrings.

#1

#2

#3

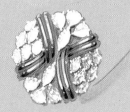

#4

#5

PLATE 80. ALL DIAMOND EARRINGS

Abandoning the use of gold, with Plate 80, we are now entering, with the diamond earring, a field where the stone's shape and size will become extremely meaningful. In order to create the various forms and their respective dynamics, we are challenged by the definite shapes of the stones themselves, varying in size but never in shape.

Among these shapes, baguettes and rounds can be grouped and set in compact elements, as in designs #4, #5 & #6. Fortunately, for the designer, a great deal of movement and volume can be obtained through the use of various stone sizes, levels, inclinations, and, in some instances, the possibility of overlapping.

Earrings #1, #2 & #3 rely mostly on the inclination and level of their stones, as well as the angles at which they are positioned. This is not to say that these factors are not present in the other designs, but, indeed, are always important when working with diamond jewelry.

#2

#1

#3

#4

#5

#6

PLATE 81. PRECIOUS COLORED GEMS & DIAMOND EARRINGS

We are now moving into a more expensive realm with the diamond and precious gemstone earring examples in Plate 81. Generally, when precious gemstones can be paired, a jeweler will consider mounting them in earrings, using diamonds for contrast and to enhance the color. Often these colored gems will be quite sizable and should, in all logic, remain the main focus of interest in the design. The designer's challenge in this type of earring is to create an attractive pattern with the surrounding diamonds, without overpowering the colored gems.

Precious gems of various color, cut and shape have been chosen to best illustrate the use of complementary diamonds in the six button earrings. The size and shape variation of the diamond contributes to the light and interesting forms and movements created within the designs. It is obvious that the differing levels also play an important part in the modeling and volume of the earrings, and this should be clearly indicated in the rendering.

PLATE 82. COLORED GEMS & DIAMOND EARRINGS

Plate 82 brings us to the colored gemstone earring, and a broader field of interpretation. While the precious gemstones generally require a more classic approach to their ornamentation, the colored gemstones lend themselves to more fantasy through a larger choice of materials and designs. Gold reappears, and with it, a combination of different colors within the same design. In some cases, diamonds will be used as a relief, a contrasting factor, displayed in most modest elements due to the need to keep the overall cost of the earrings in line with the value of the colored gemstones. The array of colored gemstones is quite impressive and, in the last two or three decades, has generated a renewed interest.

The seven earring examples, based on the use of faceted and cabochon colored gemstones, demonstrate the mixing of colors, the addition of diamonds and gold, or the use of gold without any additional stones.

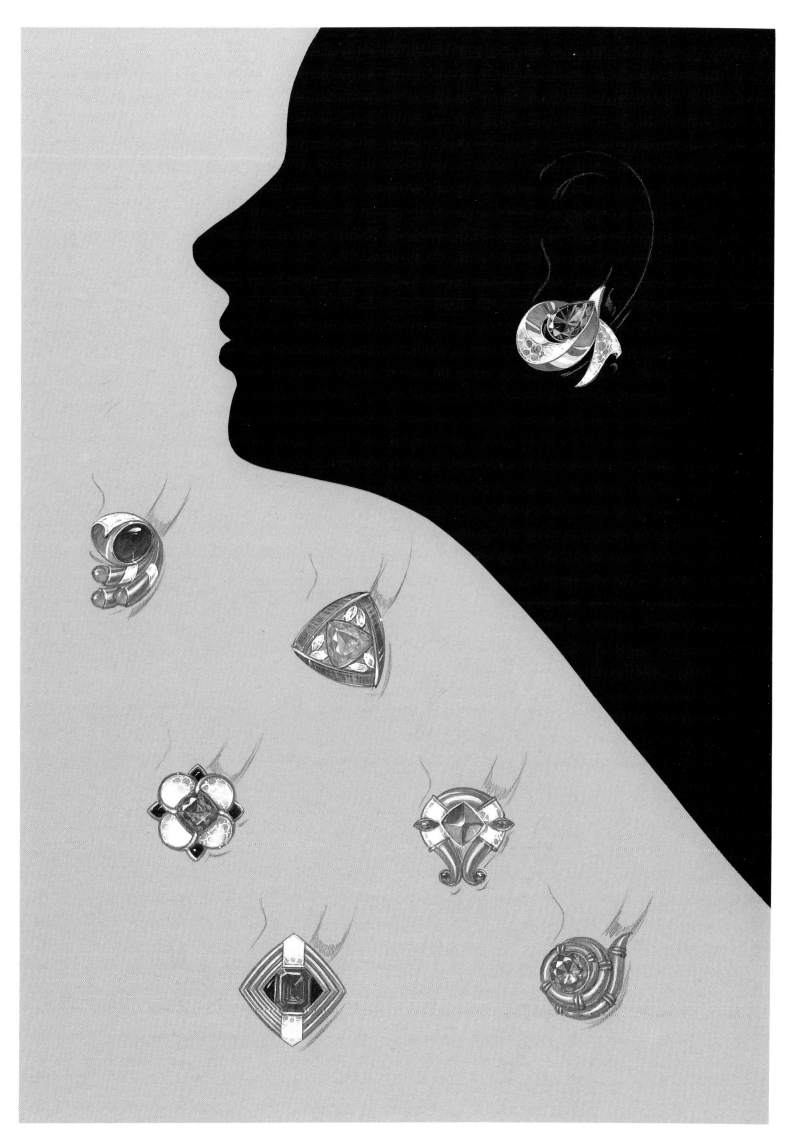

PLATE 83. SPECIAL-CUT BUTTON EARRINGS

"Special-cuts," as they are known in our trade, offer a great deal of possibilities design-wise, conforming to various shapes. Here, the designer enjoys a freedom most helpful to his or her creativeness, since the stones can be adapted to the design and not the other way around, as would be the case if working with fancies.

For the most part, one characteristic common to all special-cuts, is the "buffed-top" cut that can be described as a semi-cabochon or slightly cushioned shape - devoid of any facets. Their adaptability depends on this feature, avoiding the problems related to faceting irregular-shaped gems.

At present, jewelry using special-cuts is very much in fashion, and has been for nearly a decade, with some Italian firms literally making them part of their trade-mark.

With six designs, Plate 84 demonstrates various options for button earrings using special-cuts, with or without the addition of diamonds and gold elements, the mixing of colors meant to bring added interest to the composition. As always, the choice of materials will condition the price range of these earrings, which can be made either with precious or more moderate stones cut to specification, with the price-point being the building factor determining the choice.

PLATE 84. "INVISIBLE-SET" EARRINGS

We have become acquainted with "invisible-settings" by the previous plates dedicated to rings, and the principles applied to the ring designs are equally relevant to the earrings.

The compact look of invisibly-set jewels depends wholly on the use of substantial colored surfaces set-off by contrasting diamond elements.

In designing invisible-set motifs, one must be aware of the technical limitations inherent in this type of work, mainly the eventual problems arising from overly pointed or indented shapes, and the resulting fragility of the gems cut to fit these shapes.

Plate 84 contains five earring designs demonstrating the use of ruby, sapphire and diamond invisibly-set motifs. Diamonds have been recently added to the gems used in invisible-set jewels, and of the two types of stone-cuts calibré and princess calibré are featured in the illustration.

PLATE 85. IMPORTANT PEARL BUTTON EARRINGS.

Important pearls of fine quality warrant settings that make use of an appreciable amount of diamonds, either rounds, fancies, or baguettes. Round pearls are mostly set in button earrings, whereas drop or baroque pearls lend themselves better to pendant designs.

The diamonds are added to contrast the pearl's soft texture and supply the earring ornamentation.

Plate 85 illustrates a variety of options utilizing diamonds in motifs that include pavé and baguette "channel-set" elements, prong-set fancies, rounds and baguettes, and "scallop- set" diamonds. These motifs, whether symmetrical or asymmetrical, complement the pearls without overpowering them, and their volume is proportionate to the pearl size.

PLATE 86. TAILORED PEARL EARRINGS

The earrings illustrated in Plate 86 feature baroque and mabe pearls, as well as black and white pearls, all considerably less expensive than the types featured in Plate 85. Based on this consideration, the style of ornamentation and materials used in the designs conform to the pearl's inherent value, which at the outset determines the designer's vision.

In the illustration, gold elements of various shapes and patterns surround the pearls, either totally or partially, and others, as in the black and white pearl model, connect the pearls with a decorative "nail" element. Or, a cushion-shape design makes use of mother-of-pearl triangles to create an interesting and affordable contrast.

Compact elements create a tailored look in designs, while the use of more detailed motives can effectively complement and contrast with the mass of the pearl, as exemplified by the two bottom earrings.

PLATE 87. VARIATIONS ON A BASIC SHAPE

"Never abandon a sound concept until it has been explored to its limit." This maxim must be remembered by students and put into practice as often as possible, since it will train them to adapt a variety of materials to a single concept.

Plate 87 exemplifies a cost progression through six interpretations of a basic shape involving the use of gold, diamonds and colored gems.

PLATE 88. "SPECIAL ORDER" STUDY. BUTTON EARRING

As a rule, with "special order" work, three or four designs are sufficient for presentation to the customer, since more options have the tendency to confuse rather than to motivate a choice. Upon their first meeting, preliminary ideas are sketched by the designer based on the customer's taste and budget. Following this meeting, the full renderings will be completed and sent to the client for approval and, ultimately, will be used by the jeweler for manufacturing purposes.

The client's preference and taste is of the utmost importance to the designer, and the success of a "special order" depends to a great extent on the ability to "read" the client's mind.

Plate 88 illustrates the use of tzavorite gems and small round diamonds remounted in a button earring. Among the three designs submitted, the one chosen is checked and rendered in three steps in the lower portion of the plate.

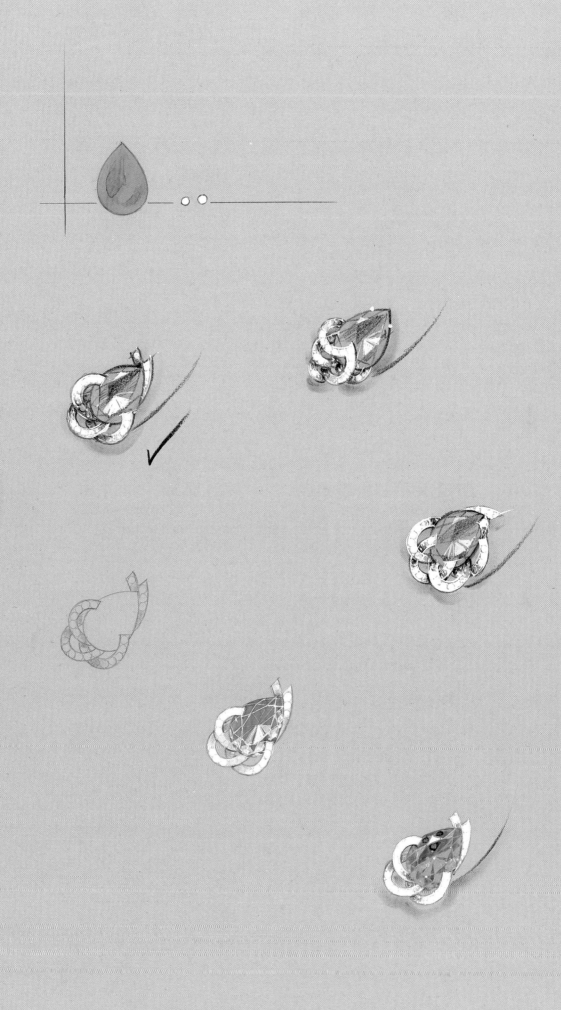

PLATE 89. GOLD HOOP EARRINGS

Among the various forms of earrings, the "hoop" has proved to be one of the most enduring styles in time, a fact confirmed by their ongoing popularity.

Plate 89 illustrates different generic hoop earrings, with single and multiple elements leading to various forms, textures, and widths. Composed either by larger compact elements or an assemblage of round wires, these designs reflect a diversity of shapes and textures, by no means limited to these models.

Countless variations could be developed where the number, size, and textures of wires can overlap, weave, or criss-cross. In addition, a further range of possibilities could be afforded by the wire shape which can be round, square, twisted, beaded, and tapered -- to name a few.

PLATE 90. GOLD AND DIAMOND HOOP EARRINGS

Plate 90 introduces an illustration of fancier and more elaborate types of hoop designs, where great freedom of interpretation is applied for inventive designs, which also include diamond details.

With the exception of the design featuring tapered baguettes, gold is the predominant material used, and the diamonds underline the gold motives and tend to make these earrings look more formal, and, therefore more wearable.

In these models, the gold motives define the overall pattern of the earring, to which the diamonds are added, completing the designs.

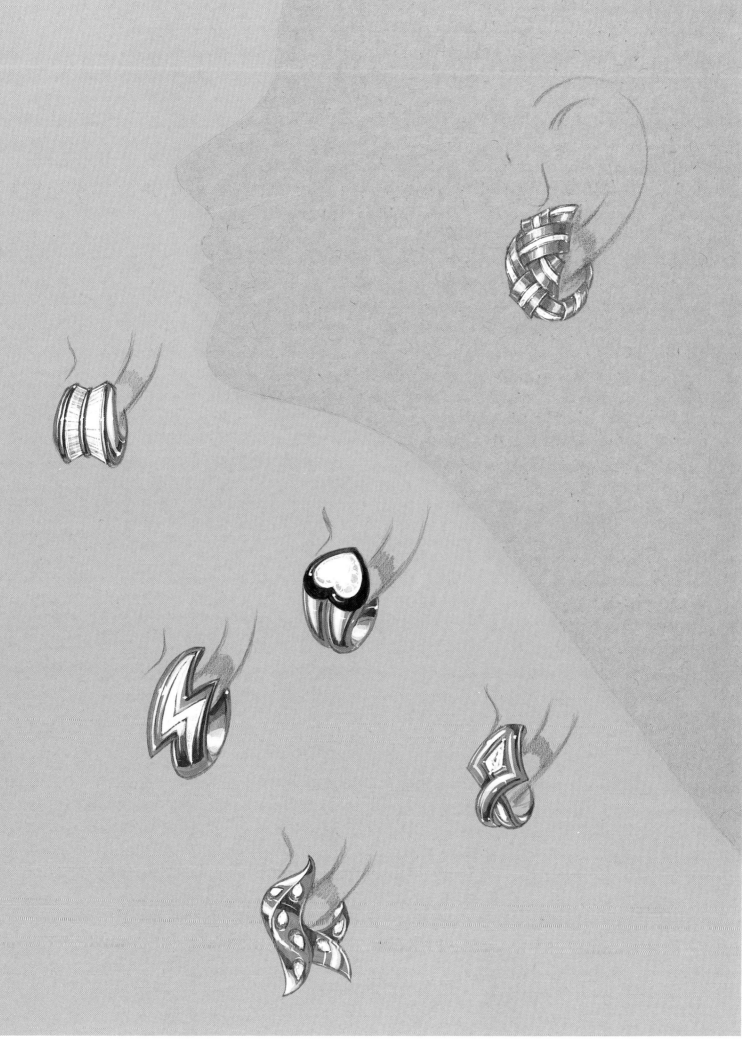

PLATE 91. PRECIOUS COLORED GEM HOOP EARRINGS

       The hoop earrings illustrated in Plate 91 feature important colored gems set in diamond mountings.

       Gold has disappeared as an ornament, and diamonds, displayed in pavé or prong-set elements, become the expected complement to these expensive gems. To maintain their predominance in the design, the colored gems are set at or slightly above the center of the hoop, and are either embedded within a pavé ornament or surrounded by fancy diamonds. Occasionally, smaller colored gems can be added to accentuate the shape of the main stone, as in the hoop example featuring an emerald with calibré sapphires.

PLATE 92. FANCY COLORED DIAMOND HOOPS

Ranking at the top of a cost progression study starting with the gold hoop, the earrings illustrated in Plates 91 and 92 are of a kind mostly available in leading jewelry companies, with the access and purchasing power to acquire gems of such size and quantity.

Based on patterns composed of graduating stones, the hoop models illustrated assemble individual diamonds into hoops of various shapes (as opposed to the previous plate, where the design is constructed around a main center stone). To add volume to the earrings, the stones are disposed at various levels and/or angles, a technique frequently used with diamond jewelry.

It is important to emphasize that in jewels of this category, the designer's involvement is always in consequence to the gem(s)'s acquisition.

PLATE 93. SPECIAL-CUT STONE HOOPS

As previously noted, the remarkable adaptability of the "special-cut" stones pertains to all types of jewels. Plate 93 shows an assortment of patterns based on a similar hoop shape demonstrating this versatility.

Visually, in all instances, the earring's surface is uniform, allowing for the maximum contrast of the special-cut stones, and the use of gold is limited to the settings.

The contrasting stone colors and the distinctive subjects for the pattern provide the interest in these designs.

PLATE 94. VARIATIONS ON A BASIC SHAPE

At this point, the student should be familiar with the type of study illustrated in Plate 94, where the sketches reflect eight variations derived from a basic shape.

Again, let us emphasize the usefulness of this study from a manufacturer's point of view, which always welcomes the opportunity to obtain a range of styles from one model at different price points.

PLATE 95. PENDANT EARRINGS

Pendant earrings are by far the most ornamental type. Modeled in gold or precious gems, casual or formal, they remain an indispensable complement to a woman's attire.

The designs in Plate 95 serve as an introduction to the subject of pendant earrings, and represent three separate concepts of: gold earrings; gold earrings with minimal diamond accents; and diamond earrings with gold accents.

The physical weight of the earrings is the only restraining factor for the design and, more importantly, to prevent an ensuing loss. Pendants should also be articulated to an extent since stiffness would cancel their elegance, especially where gems are involved. The top part of the earrings has an opposite requirement which must allow for the firm positioning of the clip (requiring a solid element) on the lobe.

The aesthetic of this type of jewel demands that the top and bottom elements be stylistically compatible, with an increase of the visual weight towards the lower section.

PLATE 96. SILVER WITH GOLD PENDANT EARRINGS

Plate 95 illustrates the combination of silver with gold accents in six earring designs. The low cost of silver affects both the styles and proportions of these earrings where, occasionally, a whimsical license is used as in the "tie" design at the bottom left of the plate.

The gold accents add both contrast and a more precious look to the otherwise silver pendants without unduly raising their cost.

PLATES 97 AND 98. COLORED GEMSTONE & DIAMOND PENDANT EARRINGS

Plate 97 and 98 feature the use of important colored stones in classic pendant earrings. Consistent with this type of earring, the greatest visual weight is placed in the bottom half, usually in a two to one proportion, either by incorporating the main stone in the pendant part, or as in the ruby "tassel" earring (of Plate 97) by the grouping of smaller colored stones in a larger element.

The examples also illustrate how the overall look is affected by the setting styles of the diamonds, compact when set in pavé elements, or delicate when set in individual prong settings. The earrings in Plate 98 introduce gold accents, giving the earrings a less formal look. For all the designs, the ability to maintain a stylistic cohesiveness between the two elements is an important aspect of the composition.

PLATE 98. COLORED GEMSTONE & DIAMOND PENDANT EARRINGS

PLATES 99 AND 100. DIAMOND PENDANT & CHANDELIER EARRINGS

The formal all-diamond earring designs in Plates 99 and 100 feature important pear shapes and emerald cuts. To best highlight these gems, smaller fancies are used either to create supple motives or entourages, while baguettes set in channels help achieve cascading effects, an ever popular look originating in the late 40's.

From a rendering point, the depth implicated in the diamond, set at different levels and angles, or overlapped, should be emphasized with a graduation of values pertaining to the volume. This aspect of rendering is particularly useful in designs without perspective where the depth relies exclusively on tonal differentiation.

Plate 99 shows a "chandelier" earring defined by the supple articulation of the elements composing the pendant part, similar to its namesake. The step by step illustration underlines the usefulness of working with structural guidelines allowing for a pleasing disposition and flexibility of the elements.

PLATE 100. DIAMOND PENDANT & CHANDEVER EARRINGS

PLATE 101. LARGE PEARL & DIAMOND PENDANT EARRINGS

Baroque and pear shaped pearls are well-suited to pendant earrings, and when available in pairs, are mainly mounted in this manner.

Plate 101 illustrates several examples. The "tassel" design places the large pearl on the top of the earring, holding a cascade of smaller pearls by a pavé cup. The flexibility afforded by the tassel attractively contrasts with the more stationary top pearl.

The "spray" design also features flexible tapered elements which contain the main pearls resulting in a similar contrast.

The design featuring two black South Sea pearls uses a contrasting pattern of alternating tapered baguettes and rounds, elongating the look of the earring while framing the pearl. The pendant pearl swings freely within its entourage.

The other models, using floral and bow motifs, are more compact with the diamonds concentrated in the top elements, resulting in a less formal look.

PLATE 102. MABE PEARL PENDANT EARRINGS

Mabe pearls are mostly of a larger diameter, 14 to 20 millimeters, and moderately priced. Used in large earrings and combined with colored stones and gold, they offer a wide range of creative possibilities as reflected in the examples of Plate 102.

While the patterns of these earrings are more exotic, when compared to the previous plate, the use of diamonds has been substituted by colorful enamel or hard stones such as jade, coral, and rock crystal, set in intricate or tailored gold motives.

PLATE 103. SPECIAL-CUT PENDANT EARRINGS

Plate 103 illustrates the previously mentioned versatility of special-cuts, in a selection of pendant earrings. The models in this plate exemplify two methods related to the use of colored gemstones in general. The first is where the colored gems are fitted or edged by diamond, or diamond & gold elements; the second is where diamond or gold are avoided, and the colored stones assume the total visual effect, either with complimentary or contrasting color schemes.

In designing jewels where the color scheme becomes the principal feature, it is important to note the following rule, which is with few exceptions applicable: *When using contrasting colors, it is most effective to limit the contrast to two colors,* as in the onyx, citrine, & tourmaline model. In the absence of contrasting colors, the palette can include a broader scheme of related or complimentary tones.

PLATE 104. VARIATIONS ON A BASIC SHAPE

Plate 104 shows a "variation on a basic shape" through six interpretations of a pendant earring. Consistent with plates and information dealing with the same theme, the similarity of these designs rests on the proportions and disposition of the elements, which all contain a top motif characterized by an upward sweep, and a pendant made of two vertical drop elements.

GLOSSARY

BALLERINA SETTING: A type of entourage mounting made of tapered baguette diamonds set in an undulating "tutu" pattern, hence its name. (pl. 46)

BEAD SET: A setting technique where the stones are held by small beads raised from the metal surrounding the stones. (pl. 47)

BEZEL SET (or closed or tube setting): A style of setting a stone by which it is fitted in a "box" made from a thin metal band or plate, covering the entire diameter of the stone. (pl. 47)

BRIGHT EDGE: A technical term referring to the edge of a bead-set jewel where the highly polished edge is achieved with a sharp cutting tool. (pl. 47)

BUFF TOP: See Special-cuts.

BAGUETTE: A cutting style, usually used for diamonds of long, narrow rectangular form featuring step-cut facets (tapered- baguette - variant of this style). (pl. 46, 168)

BRILLIANT CUT (or ROUND): A standard cut for diamonds consisting of 58 facets, 33 on the crown, and 25 on the pavilion.

BRIOLETTE: A drop of pear-shaped gem faceted over its entire surface with small triangular facets.

BAROQUE PEARL: A round or barrel shaped pearl of irregular form.

CABOCHON: A setting style where the gem has a polished domed curved surface with no facets. (pl. 39, 40)

CALIBRÉ: A square or rectangular set gem of small dimensions cut to fit a specific mount, usually with step cut facets. (pl. 46)

"CANARY" DIAMOND: A term used for diamonds of a fine yellow color. Also referred to as "fancy color" diamonds. (pl. 181, 187)

CHANDELIER: A type of earring named after the crystal chandelier fixture, it features multiple vertical elements in articulated settings. (pl. 99)

CHANNEL SET: A method by which the stone or stones are set in two tracks of metal forming a channel. Although more frequently used in conjunction with Baguette and Calibre gems, channel set can also accommodate round stones. (pl. 47, 85)

COCKTAIL (ring): A generic term applied to large gold domed rings featuring the mixing of various colored gems with diamonds. (pl. 65)

COLLERETTE: French term referring to a small round shape collar necklace. (pl. 68)

EMERALD-CUT: A form of step cutting, rectangular in shape, with the number of rows of step cuts varying. A form of cut that has a square girdle outline, but modified by corner facets.

ENTOURAGE: A type of setting or mounting used for precious gemstones, in all jewel forms, composed by a uniform or symmetrical border of stones surrounding the main gem. (pl. 63)

FANCY (CUT) DIAMOND: Any style of diamond cutting other than the round brilliant cut - including the marquise, emerald, heart shape, pear shape, keystone. Also refers to the body color of a diamond, if it is of a color other than white. Blue, red or green are the rarest. (pl. 92)

FESTOON: A curvaceous type of pattern hanging in a hoop and reminiscent of the wreaths or garlands made of flowers, leaves or other materials.

FRENCH PUFF: See Special-Cuts.

INVISIBLE-SET: A method of setting where stones are grooved under the girdle and slid on a "T" shaped rail forming a compact gem surface devoid of metal. (pl. 66, 84)

MABE PEARL: A type of cultured pearl in the form of a blister pearl obtained by cementing a spherical bead of mother of pearl to the nacreous internal surface of an oyster shell - returning the oyster to the water where the bead is quickly covered by a coat of nacre. The bead is subsequently cut off the shell and its lower part, not covered by the nacreous substance, ground off and replaced with a piece of mother of pearl. The non-nacreous base is usually covered by a closed-back setting in jewelry. (pl. 69, 102)

MARQUISE (OR NAVETTE): A cut that is a modification of the brilliant cut, so that the girdle is boat-shaped.

MINAUDIERE: A term coined by Van Cleef & Arpels, borrowed from the French "Minauder," meaning "to be, to act coquettish or coy," and given to their jeweled evening bags. (pl. 190)

MOTHER-OF-PEARL: The smooth inner lining of a mollusk's shell, composed of nacre. (pl. 69)

ORIENT: The iridescent phenomenon of a pearl. (pl. 41)

OPAQUE: Transmitting no light, even through thin edges.

PARURE (OR SET): A set of matching jewelry usually comprising a necklace, a pair of earrings, a bracelet, rings or (demi-parure - a partial set) other pieces.

PAVÉ (OR PAVÉ SETTING): A French word meaning the style of setting stones as closely as possible so that the least amount of metal shows. (pl. 44, 45)

PEAR-SHAPED: A variation of the brilliant cut but with a pear- shaped girdle.

PLATE: A trade term referring to metal in (flat) sheet form.

PIQUÉ: A term borrowed from the French referring to the positioning of diamonds at an oblique angle within a cluster of settings. (pl. 171)

POINT: In weighing diamonds, .01 of a carat, a .25-carat diamond, for instance, is said to weight 25 points, or be a 25 pointer. (pl. 44)

PRECIOUS COLORED GEMS: A categorization referring to the sapphire, emerald and ruby, the term is used to differentiate these stones from the (less expensive - more common) colored gemstones. (pl. 81, 91, 148-153, 169, 170)

PRINCESS-CUT: A square shaped stone faceted in a brilliant-cut fashion, the princess-cut is a recent addition to the diamond variety. (pl. 46, 66)

REFRACTION: The bending of light rays as they pass from one medium to another of different optical density, at angles other than perpendicular to their boundary.

REFLECTION: Rebound from a surface. Light which strikes a reflecting surface is reflected at the same angle to the normal as the angle of incidence.

SCALLOP SET: A style of setting specific to round gems where the stones are bezel set in an element forming an ornamental edge made of a series of curves.

SIGNET RING: A type of man's ring that has an engraved insignia either in metal or in a bezel-set hard stone. (pl. 50, 72)

SOLITAIRE (RING OR ENGAGEMENT): A type of ring consisting of a single stone set in a platinum or gold prong setting mounted on a single shank. The solitaire is the traditional engagement ring. (pl. 52, 53, 54)

SPECIAL-CUTS: (Buff Top, French Puff) A recent cutting style applied to color gemstones when the gem is cut and polished in a low domed cabochon shape without any facets. (pl. 40, 70, 83, 93, 103, 147, 166)

SPECIAL ORDER: A trade term referring to an order where specific gemstones are involved and furnished by the customer. (pl. 71, 88)

STEP-CUT: A cutting technique where the area below the table has a varying number of sloping parallel rows of straight facets which give the impression of steps.

STRAIGHT BAR (OR GEMLOCK SETTING): A setting style where the stones are secured on either side by a metal strip. (pl. 47)

TIARA: Of ancient Persian origin, the term "tiara" designates a woman's crown-like headdress of jewels adorning the forehead (frontal area of the face). (pl. 186, 187)

TRANSLUCENT: Transmitting light but diffusely. Example: frosted glass.

TRANSPARENT: Transmitting light with a minimum of distortion.

SELECTED BIBLIOGRAPHY FOR GLOSSARY:

Dickenson, J.Y., The Book of Diamonds. Crown. NY 1965
Mascetti, D., & Triossi, A. Earrings From Antiquity to the Present. Rizzoli. London 1990.
Liddicoat, R., Handbook on Gem Identification. G.I.A., CA 1989.

SUGGESTED BOOKS:

Schumann, W., Gemstones of the World. England 1977
Way, M. Perspective Drawing. London 1989.
Untracht, O. Jewelry Concepts and Technology. N.Y. 1985

In addition to books on jewelry, we suggest referring to books on decorative arts, ornament, architecture, textile design and nature.

Illustration Credits

Maurice P. Galli

Plates: 5, 7, 11, 15, 19, 24, 27, 29, 32, 33, 34, 35, 37, 38, 39, 42, 43, 44, 48, 53, 54, 58, 59, 67, 72, 74, 75, 76, 78, 79, 81, 88, 92, 96, 98, 99, 100, 104

Dominique Rivière

Plates: 1, 2, 3, 4, 6, 8, 9, 17, 21, 23, 25, 28, 30, 36, 45, 46, 47, 49, 51, 52, 55, 56, 61, 62, 63, 64, 66, 71, 73, 82, 89, 90, 91, 94, 95, 97

Fanfan Li

Plates: 10, 12, 13, 14, 16, 18, 20, 22, 26, 31, 40, 41, 50, 57, 65, 68, 69, 70, 77, 80, 83, 84, 85, 86, 87, 93, 101, 102, 103

About the Authors:

Professor Maurice P. Galli teaches Jewelry Design at the Fashion Institute of Technology in New York City. For the past forty-eight years, his work experience has involved positions at Harry Winston, David Webb, and Van Cleef & Arpels. He currently manages the Jewelry Design Department at Tiffany & Company, where he has been employed for the past seventeen years.

Born in Cannes, France, Maurice obtained his C.A.P. from the Chambre Syndicale de la Bijouterie, Joaillerie et Orfevrerie de Paris. He has followed a family tradition; his father had owned a jewelry store in Cannes, and his grandfather was a master jeweler and manufacturer in Florence, Italy. Professor Galli resides in New York, where his daughter, Myriam Galli, also works in the jewelry business involved with sales and promotion at Gemveto.

Fanfan Li, a designer at Van Cleef & Arpels, New York, has been working with the firm since she graduated from The Fashion Institute of Technology in New York in 1989. That same year, she won both the Van Cleef & Arpels Young Designer's Scholarship and the Young Creator Award sponsored by the Comité Colbert.

Fanfan was born in China in 1958, where she was raised in a family of artists and writers who inspired her orientation. She studied Fine Arts and apprenticed under Yu Gi Gao, as master of traditional Chinese painting, in Nan Jing, before graduating from the Anshan Jiao Nai Design and Research Institute. She worked as an architect prior to moving to New York.

Dominique Rivière is currently the head designer at Gemveto Inc., a jewelry manufacturer in New York, whose clients include such firms as Tiffany & Co. He was born in France in 1948, and graduated from the Chambre Syndicale de la Bijouterie, Joaillerie et Orfevrerie de Paris where he originally received formal training as a jeweler before concentrating on design. Dominique began his career in Paris working for the manufacturer Guillemin-Soulaine, who supplied such well-known jewelers as Cartier, Harry Winston, and Mouawad (in Saudi Arabia).

Dominique moved to New York in 1984, and met his wife Fanfan in 1989, with whom he shares a passion for jewelry, thus uniting the cultures of Europe, Asia, and America.